Praise for
Untying Parent Anxiety

"As a real dad of two boys and a TV dad of three, I know the unrealistic expectations facing today's parents. Everyone's shooting for perfection. But in *Untying Parent Anxiety*, Lisa reminds us that screwing up is the only thing we can really count on. And that's good by me, because perfect's not that much fun for anyone."

—Andy Buckley, actor, star of *Odd Mom Out* and
The Office, father of two

"Through humor, street smarts and life experience, Ms. Sugarman presents a relatable, easily applicable "how to" coping manual that any parent can reference during those tense parenting moments we all face. *Untying Parent Anxiety* normalizes challenges that most people face and offers level-headed, every-day practical responses that lets the reader feel like they aren't alone."

—Melissa Kaplowitch, PhD, Counseling Psychology Professor,
Salem State University, mom of three

"Navigating this crazy thing called parenthood is a little easier with Lisa on your side."

—Kathy Doody, General Manager of
Being a Mom.life, mom of three

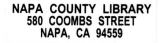

"Lisa's writing is hilarious. She delivers parenting advice without judgement, in a light, witty way that makes the reader feel like it's coming from a good friend."

—Lauren Fowler, Manager, Spirit of '76 Bookstore

"Lisa Sugarman has finally put out to the universe what every parent needs to hear but what every teacher and pediatrician can't get away with saying. Kids need to be kids above all. Lisa does a stellar job highlighting how to not just let a kid be a kid but explains how parents can swiftly and responsibly teach our children how to live balanced, responsible, and happy lives full of it all: chores, electronics, social media, and more! This is a must-read if you really want to learn the truth about not just being a good parent but a happy one too!"

—Debra Fox Gansenberg, MSW, LICSW,
Co-Founder and Director of School Services,
New Beginnings Counseling Service, P.C., mom of three

"There really is no manual for parenting. I could use a step-by-step, year-by-year, drama-by-drama handbook, and Lisa Sugarman is the only person who's come close to delivering one. She single-handedly makes you feel human, like you can still breathe, and like there's still hope for you as a parent. Do you know the type of writing you never want to stop reading? The kind that makes you upset when a chapter or a book ends? Lisa Sugarman does that to me. Every. Single. Time."

—Courtney Monaco, mom of two

"Thank you, thank you, thank you, Lisa. As a mom of two active, and we'll say 'savvy' young men, parenting can occasionally feel like a swirling vortex of doom: too many decisions, too many different ways to tack, and too much to do. But you've broken it down beautifully and given me my new mantra geared to raising good people: Be Consistent. Stay on Task. Allow for Imperfections. And Love the Ride."

—Kelly Calnan, mom of two

"Lisa's perspective is so reassuring and spot on—and practical. Reading her work is 100% like being able to pull your sage girlfriend off the bookshelf on a whim and tap into her expertise. The sections about screens and about chores? I was high-fiving her with my mind."

—Alison Carey, mom of four

UNTYING

Parent Anxiety

Published by Familius LLC, www.familius.com

Familius books are available at special discounts for bulk purchases, whether for sales promotions or for family or corporate use. For more information, contact Familius Sales at 559-876-2170 or email orders@familius.com.

Library of Congress Cataloging-in-Publication Data
2016959872

Print ISBN 9781944822576
Ebook ISBN 9781944822590
Hardcover ISBN 9781944822583

Printed in the United States of America

Edited by DeAnna Acker
Cover design by David Miles
Book design by Brooke Jorden

10 9 8 7 6 5 4 3 2 1

First Edition

Years
5-8

UNTYING

Parent Anxiety

18 Myths that
Have You in Knots—
And How to Get Free

LISA SUGARMAN

. . . because we're only as happy as our least happy kid.

For my family. Because
you're my Dream Team.
No one loves you like I do.

XO

Contents

Preface

I'm around kids a lot. A whole lot. Between working in an elementary school for the last ten years plus and mothering my two daughters, I spend an awful lot of time with kids (and parents) every day. And what I see, more and more often, are kids cracking under the pressure of their parents' unrealistic expectations—expectations that they outdo their peers in every conceivable way.

As a result, kids are seeing specialists in record numbers and being medicated to control everything from anxiety disorders and depression to social phobias and panic attacks. And I see it all firsthand every day. According to the Child Mind Institute's *2016 Children's Mental Health Report*, 17.1 million young people under the age of eighteen have or have had a diagnosable psychiatric disorder.[1] And that number continues to rise. In fact, YoungMinds.org reported as recently as 2013 that the number of young people aged fifteen to sixteen with depression nearly doubled between the 1980s and the 2000s.[2] Scary statistics if you're a parent.

I've spent almost two decades watching kids and parents fall apart around me when they didn't make the team or win MVP or get into their first-choice Ivy League college. And let me tell you, it's gut wrenching, because these kids can't cope with anything less than perfection . . . and neither can their parents.

You've noticed, I'm sure, that helicopter parents are everywhere, with kids being so micromanaged by hypercompetitive moms and dads that they have no time left just to be kids. I'll bet, without even thinking twice, you can rattle off a list of parents you know who are overscheduling their kids so that every available second of their day is filled with activities. You may even be doing some of it yourself without realizing it.

As the author of the nationally syndicated opinion column *It Is What It Is* and the *Boston Globe* local bestseller *LIFE: It Is What It Is*, I've spent the last eight years reminding people that **life is always a work in progress**—that no one's perfect and we're not supposed to be. Especially kids. And I've decided that what today's parents need more than anything is a wake-up call to dial down their intensity and let their kids just be kids while they can. And if that means making some mistakes along the way, then so be it.

Because, in my opinion, too many parents today have forgotten that one of the most important skills we can impart to our children is the ability to screw up and still keep moving forward. And that's because this idea of being perfect just isn't realistic—not for us as adults, or for our kids, as we all navigate our very imperfect world.

Until now, though, there's never been a parenting book devoted to teaching parents to lighten up as a way of getting more out of their kids. So that's why I wrote *Untying Parent Anxiety: 18 Myths That Have You in Knots—And How to Get Free* as a resource that reminds parents to set the bar at a reasonable height for their kids. Because if they set it too high from the get-go, their kids will never have a shot at clearing it.

Along with Dave, my husband of almost twenty-five years, I've weathered every stage of parenthood, from finding that little red plus sign on the pregnancy test to sending my oldest off to college. And I'm still standing. And so are our kids. And what I've learned through it all is that life—**especially parenting**—is never the straight line we imagine it to be when we're starting out. Instead, parenting is an uneven road, pitted with oversized sinkholes and full of detours we never expect. But it's also one helluva beautiful ride. We just need to accept that we're not going to be perfect parents and our kids aren't going to be perfect kids. And that's okay, because we're not supposed to be. Because by giving our kids the tools to accept failure, we can actually do more to help unlock their true potential than you'd ever imagine.

With *Untying Parent Anxiety*, you'll be able to commiserate, laugh, and cry with someone who's wading through the same day-to-day muck that you are. I'll share some of my proudest mama moments, some of my heartbreaks, and some of my challenges and my triumphs and help you understand why one of the best things we can do for our kids—and ourselves—is take a step back and give them the reins. Because, sometimes, the most valuable gift we can give our kids is the ability to let them help themselves. That's where the real magic happens.

And the sooner you embrace that, the better off you'll all be.

Introduction

How do you raise *the perfect child?*

Loaded question, isn't it? The answer is simple, though. *You don't.* Sorry.

Yet parents everywhere continue to try to raise their kids to be smarter, faster, more successful, and more popular than their peers. They're bringing them up to believe that failure is not an option, oblivious that what they're actually doing is setting them up to crash and burn.

As the mom of two girls—a junior in high school and a sophomore in college—I know it's not easy to go from zero to six hundred overnight when we become parents. But that's just what parenthood is—the ultimate baptism by fire. One day it's just you and your deliciously warm down comforter sleeping in on a cold Sunday morning, and then it's not. Before you know it, you've got little ones hopping onto your bed at five o'clock in the morning, prying open your eyelids and begging for pancakes. And then you're "on" until one of you loses steam twelve to eighteen hours later.

But at the very same time that parenthood upends our lives in every possible way, it also starts us on the most beautiful journey that most of us will ever know. And like most journeys, it's much easier to navigate when we have some sort of a road map to at least guide us in the right direction. Just enough help to ensure that we don't stray too far off course.

That's why I wrote *Untying Parent Anxiety*—to help you stay on course and to give you a glimpse of what lies ahead so you can avoid the pitfalls of trying to be the perfect parent and raise the perfect kid.

Because in case you haven't noticed, most maps are one-dimensional representations of the real world. They don't give us the *local knowledge* we really need to get around. You know, the kind of information that shows us where all the bumps are and how to avoid them. Something that only a local would know.

Well, I'm your local. And *Untying Parent Anxiety* is your new source for all the local knowledge you'll need to help you stay nimble when you hit unexpected detours along the way. In it, I address everything from social and emotional growth to cognitive development and all the major developmental milestones in between. I break things down into short, manageable chapters that highlight the **myths** and the **truths** of parenting and remind you what's *really* important in terms of raising emotionally healthy kids—and what's not.

Why, though, does the book start at age five, when our kids start kindergarten, and not when our babies are first born? That's easy—because babies are perfect, and aside from the issue of constant sleep deprivation, infancy is the easiest stage we go through as parents. Babies eat, they sleep, they poop, and they cry. End of story. And while they do evolve into crawlers and babblers and table-food eaters along the way, they don't truly start becoming their own unique little selves until they start walking and talking and getting a little taste of independence. And the most obvious mile marker for that is when they begin kindergarten. Which, of course, is when our kids *really* start learning how to push our buttons.

So think of *Untying Parent Anxiety* as a personal floatation device to keep you from drowning in all the parenting pressure around you and from pulling your kids down with you. Use it as a constant reminder that life with kids is chaotic, even on the best of days, but learning to be flexible with whatever life throws at us is our biggest asset as parents.

Whether you're a new, expectant, or experienced parent, *Untying Parent Anxiety* will reinforce the idea that our goal as parents shouldn't be to raise perfect kids but instead to raise well-adjusted little people who can handle whatever life throws at them with grace, courage, and a great sense of humor.

Now let's do this!

How to Use This Book

Since parents of young kids barely have time to zip up their fly or blow-dry their hair most days, it made sense to me to write a book that moms and dads could digest quickly, read on the fly, and utilize to find some useful nuggets of advice and wisdom to keep them centered and grounded during the day-to-day grind. That's why *Untying Parent Anxiety* is organized into bite-size chunks that you can read while you're waiting in the school pickup line or sitting in the bleachers watching soccer practice or during a quick coffee break. Stash it by your bed or in the car or even in the bathroom, and read it when you need a little infusion of sanity. Because sometimes all you need is a friendly dope slap that parenthood just isn't a straight line—and it's not supposed to be.

Myth #1

Myth: Good grades are what matter most.

Reality: Kindergarten is where our kids learn all their basic life skills.

You've heard the saying a million times, I'm sure: *Everything your kids need to know they learn in kindergarten.* And you may or may not have given it any real thought. Until now. But as far as I'm concerned, that statement is spot-on true, true, TRUE! (Well, for the most part, anyway.)

As a mom who's already experienced kindergarten with two different kids—and all the grades that come after—I can assure you that out of all the years of school my girls have cycled through, kindergarten was the most significant, bar none. And here's why . . .

It's unlikely that your son will graduate from his kindergarten class knowing that E=mc² and why. (Although, if he does, then you might want to consider sending him directly to second grade. Maybe third.) But it *is* realistic to expect that most kids will leave kindergarten decidedly more prepared for life than they were when they went in. And that's because, when you really break it down, the skills that our kids learn— that we learned—in that first real year of school are among the most essential life skills any of us needs as we move through our life.

Think about it—by the time most kids graduate on to first grade, they will have learned the alphabet, how to write words and simple sentences, how to count and share, how to name shapes and sort and classify objects, how to tell time, how to name the seasons, and, most importantly, how to work collaboratively with the people around them. And all in roughly 180 days, which is some pretty epic learning, if you ask me.

Now, granted, some kids will arrive on their first day of kindergarten already knowing a lot of this stuff or, at the very least, knowing some, but the majority of these skills will either be learned or honed during the ten months they spend in that first year of school. And it's these fundamental *life skills* that lay the foundation for everything that comes after. Like, everything. And that's a good thing. A great thing, actually. Because all of these little daily nuances they're learning in the classroom—like manners and sharing and respect—will eventually trickle into their lives at home. And that makes our job a lot easier because our kids are being reinforced by someone other than us.

Ask anyone who's spent any real time around young kids, especially in a kindergarten classroom, how quickly they sponge up all the information around them, and they'll tell you it's mind blowing. And I've watched it all firsthand.

For years, when my own kids were in elementary school, I worked as an aide in a kindergarten classroom. And, honestly, the transformation I saw in those kids over the course of just that one year was astonishing. That's because so many of them enter kindergarten in September incapable of something as simple as sitting quietly in circle time or transitioning from arts and crafts to music. But by June, most of them have evolved to a place where they can transition successfully between activities, work collaboratively with their teachers and their peers, and think creatively. And this is exactly why kindergarten is such a critical year for our kids—because it teaches them the basic skills they need to adjust to being out in the real world.

I'm talking about the exact same stuff that Robert Fulghum talked about in his *New York Times* bestseller from the '80s, *All I Really Need to Know I Learned in Kindergarten*.

I mean, when you get right down to it, Fulghum was a real visionary. He believed that "wisdom was not at the top of the graduate-school mountain, but there in the sandpile at Sunday School." He said that "everything you need to know is in there somewhere."[3] And I, for one, think he's absolutely right.

Read his list below of some of the skills he learned while he was in kindergarten. Then apply each one to your daily life, whether it's your home life, your life as a parent, or your professional life, and see for yourself how each and every one of them translates into your everyday life.

- Share everything.
- Play fair.
- Don't hit people.
- Clean up your own mess.
- Don't take things that aren't yours.
- Say you're sorry when you hurt somebody.

And if you don't believe him, the folks at the Media Lab at the Massachusetts Institute of Technology (MIT) feel the same way too. They think that we should make the rest of school (like all the grade levels)—and life—more like kindergarten.

According to a 2009 article in Edutopia.org, the MIT guys see it this way: "As kindergartners playfully create stories, castles, and paintings with one another, they develop and refine their abilities to think creatively and work collaboratively, precisely the abilities most needed to achieve success and satisfaction in the 21st century."[4]

To be honest, most of the adults I know aren't too far ahead of the kindergarteners I know. And that's because a lot of them have forgotten that it's the basic people skills we learned when we were young that are the very foundation on which our adult lives and interactions are built.

That's why it's so important that you keep cool if everything doesn't click for your kids right away when they begin school. Because, believe me, it won't. And you, as the parent, need to avoid falling into the trap of measuring your children up against all the other kids around them. You know, the ones in the other guided reading groups reading higher-level books, or your daughter's friend who did more sit-ups during the Presidential Physical Fitness Test, or your son's classmate whose artwork got picked to hang in the school lobby. Because everything comes out in the wash. They all find their own groove and settle into their own stride at their own pace. Which is *exactly* what they're supposed to do. It's what we *all* have to learn to do. And the sooner we learn it, the better off we'll be.

During that first exposure to school, our kids have enough pressure on them just learning to separate from us every day, trying to fit into a different routine, and being introduced to so many new people and experiences. So the very *last* thing they need is for us to be stacking them up against their peers and judging how they're adjusting. Because I'll give you one guess what that creates. Yup, it causes stress. And it builds tension and anxiety for us as well as for them.

And when we're stressed, no matter how hard we try to hide it, our kids sense it. They have the uncanny ability to see right through us most of the time, especially when what we're trying to conceal is about them. A lot like how our house pets can sense when there's fear or sadness or illness. And they react to it. Kids are almost exactly the same (except for the shedding).

Once we cross over into that world of using other kids as benchmarks, we stop appreciating what our own kids have to offer. So consider this a warning, because once you start openly comparing your kids to the ones around them, that's exactly what they'll start doing, and there are few things that can be more damaging to growing children than constantly measuring themselves against other people. It's exhausting, it's pointless, and it can create a seriously insecure kid.

Remember, in school, like in life, there's always going to be someone better, stronger, smarter, and faster than us. And our kids. So to accept that early on as parents will alleviate more frustration than you can imagine. Letting go of expectations frees everyone from getting caught trying to measure up.

Once you accept that every child is different and they all operate on their own unique developmental clock, you're ahead of the game. Because tampering with your child's clock too much by putting unrealistic pressure or expectations on them will be disastrous. But encouraging them to be true to themselves will show them that you've got their back and support their decisions. And when our kids feel supported, the sky is usually the limit.

See, **there's a fine line between encouragement and pressure**, and it's our job as parents to stay on the right side of that line. Because once you start telling your kids which sport to play or what instrument to choose or what language to study or which girls they should be friends with, then you've taken away their ability to figure things out for themselves. And that's bad. Then you're not encouraging them to do what's good for them. Instead, you're persuading them to do what's good for you. And that's even worse.

The other thing we need to avoid (at all costs) that's just as important as not measuring our kids up against other kids is not measuring *ourselves* against other parents. Because believe me, you'll want to. A lot. Especially once your kids get to school and you're exposed to all types of parents. Don't give in, though, if you can help it, because comparing yourself to other parents will make you crazy. It'll make you second-guess every decision you make.

And it's hard, I know, because once you start interacting with other parents and kids on a day-to-day basis, like you do once they start their school career, the temptation is high to measure yourself and your own parenting style against all the other parents you meet. That's because, at school, you learn just how many different types of parenting styles there are out there, which inevitably leads us to question how we parent our own kids. You'll catch yourself trying to adapt all the approaches other parents use, expecting that you'll have the same results. And while some will work, others will fail. Miserably.

Once we open our eyes to the world around us—in this case, the kindergarten world—we start to question whether we're being strict enough or loose enough with our kids, and that questioning leads to making bad parenting decisions based solely on how something worked for someone else. So you need to resist the urge to follow along. Because not everything works for everyone. Every child and parent and family is decidedly different.

Just remember, as you start this long and beautiful journey, that the learning curve for us as parents is almost as broad as it is for our kids. **There's no perfect path**. And the greatest thing we can do for our kids is celebrate them for who they are as unique and beautiful little people and support them as they try to find their way. And that means giving them the slack they need to explore everything around them. It means giving them the latitude to fall and to fail and to choose, on their own, what appeals to them. Can you guide them? Absolutely. Should you drive the bus for them? Absolutely not.

You've got a long way to go as you watch your kids grow and mature and work their way through the next twelve-plus years of school. I've watched my own girls stumble and fall and cry tears of joy and pain as they both tried to find their way, so I know how hard it can be as a parent to stay put on the sidelines and watch them play the game. It can be gut wrenching. You have to, though. Because empowering them when they're young to make their own decisions and handle the consequences of their actions is one of the greatest gifts we can give our kids.

And it all starts here in kindergarten. So take each little piece of it as it comes. Don't freak out if your kindergartener doesn't come home with all As—uh, I mean, check pluses—on his first report card. We need to remember that he's learning so much more than what's in a book. There are a lot of moving parts associated with kindergarten, and not all of them can be quantified on a report card. Encourage your kids to try on lots of hats and see which ones fit best for them. They'll thank you for it later on down the line, I promise. (Just don't let them try on actual hats, because lice runs pretty rampant in kindergarten.)

Myth #2

Myth: My kid will never make it out in the real world without me.

Reality: It's never too early to start letting go.

N ow I'm not suggesting that your kindergartener or first grader open a checking account and start renting a loft apartment in the next town. We're not there yet; don't worry. Because at that age, most kids barely know how to tie their own shoes, let alone how to take care of themselves in the real world. They're just little peanuts, and they're standing just on the outermost edge of their first taste of independence as they head off to school for the first time.

But what you, the parent, need to remember is that baby steps become big strides quicker than you can imagine. So if you're still holding their hand when they should be standing on their own two feet, you run the giant risk of raising a child who can't think for herself. Because then, to be blunt, you're screwed. And so are they.

See, it's not easy to predict when our kids are ready to do certain things on their own. That's because each child is unique and hits certain milestones at different times. But the more opportunities we give our kids to think and act for themselves, the more independent they become. And the more independent they become, the more self-confident and resilient they are in the long run.

Encouraging our children to **own** certain responsibilities—even the little ones—is how we raise them to have healthy self-esteem. Because there's no greater feeling to a child than being able to depend on themselves. But to do that, we need to give our kids expectations. Small ones to start, of course, like clearing their dishes and throwing their dirty clothes in the hamper. And then, eventually, we move on to the bigger tasks, like walking the dog and taking out the trash. And so on.

That's why, once our kids hit kindergarten, it's the perfect opportunity to start giving them a modest amount of slack to start taking ownership of their little lives. And at this age, that means encouraging them to do the little things: starting homework on their own and cleaning up their workspace and hanging up their own coat. Because by letting them do these small yet significant things, we're saying to them, *We know you've got this, honey. We know that you're ready for what lies ahead.* And believe me, it's those tiny acts of independence that jet-propel our kids to the next level of autonomy—autonomy that can't be reached if you're hovering over your daughter in the school lobby every morning, keeping her from branching out and connecting with new friends. If you're always the one picking out what your son is wearing every morning, then he'll never learn to dress himself. That autonomy can't be reached if you're like some parents I see three times a week dropping off forgotten water bottles and mittens and homework assignments. (Schools! Have! Drinking fountains!) No one's going to die of thirst because they don't have their BPA-free water bottle. And if your son gets cold at recess, he'll remember his gloves the next time. And your daughter won't flunk out of kindergarten because she left her "Signs of Spring" worksheet at home. This is when they need to start thinking for themselves. And this is when we let them.

If our kids know *we* believe in them, then they'll start believing in themselves. They'll start to think and act independently because we've given them the confidence to take chances and loosen their grip a little. And that's essential. Because I'm telling you, you *don't* want to be That Mom who walks your son into his first job interview. That's why it's a good idea to use the transition to kindergarten as a mile marker for introducing the concept of independence to our kids. It's the perfect time to empower them to learn to stand alone as they really start navigating the world around them.

Remember, teaching our kids how to be successful at doing grown-up tasks builds confidence. It lays the groundwork for all of the more complicated adult stuff that comes later in life, like relationships, driving, and, eventually, a career. And it's these tiny gestures of trust on our part that help put them on the path to becoming independent learners and thinkers. It also creates a sense of pride in being able to do things for themselves. And that motivates kids to want to do more and more for themselves. I guess you could call it a domino effect, because one successful accomplishment creates a feeling of pride and that feeling of pride usually leads to the desire to do more things independently, which is *exactly* what you want.

That's why, as hard as it is to do initially, it's vital that we take small opportunities, early on, to let our kids feel what it's like to be separated from us, to depend on other people, and, most importantly, to rely on themselves. And it's just as crucial for us to start the long and painstaking process of loosening our grip. But believe me: it's necessary.

After working in the school system for more than a decade, I've seen some pretty outrageous examples of parents who couldn't let go. You know them; they're the *helicopter parents* who take overprotectiveness to a sickening level. They're constantly by their child's side, they're carrying their backpack for them, they're building the shoebox diorama and speaking for them instead of letting them speak for themselves. And let me tell you, the only thing that behavior does is raise a child who can't let go. That's because, whether you realize it yet or not, our kids take their social and emotional cues from us. If they smell fear or sadness on us as we drop them off at school, the chances are good that they're going to mimic that same fear and sadness. If they see us peeking out from behind the bushes next to the kindergarten door, you can bet cash money that they're not going inside without a fight. Because if we're not willing to leave them, they're certainly not going to be willing to leave us.

I know that none of us is ever ready to step back and let our kids drive the bus. Especially after being joined at the hip for the first five or so years of their life. Dave and I were petrified when our first daughter went off to kindergarten. Watching her walk through that door for the first time, like a little Sherpa, carrying all of her own supplies and gear, put a giant lump in both our throats. It's a bittersweet moment, for sure.

I remember trying so hard to bite back the tears and stop my bottom lip from twitching just so she didn't catch onto how sad I was to see her go. But inside, I was dying. The closer she got to the classroom door, the harder it got for me to hide the thick lump of emotion rising in my throat. For me, it was like a mini life-flashing-before-my-eyes kind of moment.

It was so hard to know what to do that first time, her looking too cute for words dressed in her little denim skirt and red top with her monogrammed big-girl backpack. Did we both walk her up the hill? (Yes, we did.) Did we hold her hand? (One on either side.) Did I cry like a sentimental loser when she walked through the classroom door? (Yup, did that too.) Would her lunch stay cold? Would she remember how to tie her shoe if it came undone? Would she forget me during those six long hours? I was pathetic. But little did I know that all of my friends were thinking the exact same things.

In that split second when I kissed her goodbye and watched her pair up with another girl in her class, I saw her as a newborn, then doing her first commando crawl, then as a toddler, then a tiny little person who could zip her own coat and tie her own shoes.

On the walk back to the car, Dave tried to console me while I rattled off a flurry of crazy mom talk, like, *Well, now what?! Now what am I supposed to do?! She doesn't need me anymore. Did you see all those little girls running up to play with her in the playground? She's not even gonna remember me at pickup [heavy sobs]*. (Side note: hormones make mothers go slightly insane.)

See, on the one hand, we know that they're ready to make that transition, ready to start following a routine, and ready to start acclimating to life at school. But on the other hand, the idea is terrifying because it means letting go. And no new parent wants to do that. Because if our kids aren't with us, then we can't protect them, and protecting our kids is our number one responsibility as parents, right? Of course it is, but it's by no means our only responsibility.

Equal to protecting our kids is our job to teach them the skills and give them the wherewithal to be able to protect themselves and thrive when they're finally out from under our roof. But in order to do that, we need to know when to step in and when to step aside—a skill that happens only by trial and error. And it doesn't happen overnight. Everyone—both us and our kids—needs to wade into the water one toe at a time so we can adjust to the new world around us.

Let's face it: we live in a crazy, unpredictable world—a world that's decidedly different from the world we grew up in when we were kids. You remember what it was like when we were kids: people left their front doors open at night and their cars unlocked, and we played outside from sunup to sundown. And our moms and dads didn't even know where we were most of the time, sometimes for half the day. Life was simpler. There was no social media threatening the safety and well-being of our kids. No internet predators. No peanut-free lunch tables to consider. There were no weekly school shootings. In a lot of ways, life was less complicated. So as the mother of two daughters, I get how scary it is to anticipate my girls going out into the world. Because letting them go means giving up a certain amount of control, and that can be traumatic for parents. But learning to let go also means inspiring our kids to take charge, to take ownership, and to handle adversity—skills that are essential to their survival on their own.

And the first time most of us start laying the foundation for that independence is during our child's first few years of school. See, it's during this time, when they are away from us for a few hours a day, that our kids slowly begin to learn how to take care of themselves—a skill that they'll have to draw on time and time again as they travel through life. Because as much as we'd love to be there every step of the way, the fact is that we can't be after a certain point. We have to let them roam free-range, at least a little.

When you think about it, we're actually teaching our kids to learn to take care of themselves from the minute we bring our squishy little nuggets home from the hospital. And that never stops. We put the squeaky toy just out of their reach to encourage them to start crawling; we put piles of Cheerios on their high chair tray to allow them to feed themselves; we talk to them incessantly, helping them build a vocabulary so that, ultimately, they can learn to communicate with actual words.

You remember yourself at five or six or seven, right? Well, I do, and if you're anything like me, you remember how heavily you relied on your mom and dad. For everything. They were our caregivers and babysitters and playmates and providers. And, most of all, they were our protectors. But remember when you first started doing things on your own? Like when you got to stay home alone for the first time without a babysitter? Or when you got to use the stove for the first time? Or when you became the babysitter? Those milestones were big. Huge, in fact. And on some level, either consciously or unconsciously, we were grateful for their vote of confidence.

So that's what we have to do as our kids make this move to kindergarten: we need to give them the independence that they're already starting to crave. And even though it's their teacher who sets the bar for performing little day-to-day routines and tasks at school, like hanging up their coat and unpacking their backpack and remembering to zip their fly before they leave the bathroom, it's our job to reinforce all of the independent skills they're learning when our kids are back on our turf. Actually, it's crucial. Because if everyone is consistent with their expectations, then our kids begin to learn and anticipate what's expected of them. (Key word there is *anticipate*.) And that's a big concept because it enables our kids to understand how they're supposed to handle themselves in school and at home and out in the rest of the world.

So the upshot of all this: while it's obviously not time to kick our kids to the curb and have them fend for themselves, it's definitely time to start giving them a little extra latitude so they can begin to think and do for themselves. Because that's the way we raise healthy, independent kids.

Myth #3

Myth: Drop-off disasters are inevitable.

Reality: Saying goodbye at drop-off won't always be an ugly mess.

In Myth #2, we talked about letting go so our kids can learn a little independence and how school can play a big role in that learning process. But that means getting used to an entirely new routine—a routine that, for many, involves spending almost as much time away from each other as you spend together. And adapting to that separation is never simple, not for us or for our kids.

Giving our kids the right amount of space to develop a sense of independence and to learn to think for themselves is usually much easier said than done. But it *is* possible, and it's very, very necessary. And knowing how to separate is a big step toward making that happen.

So the question then becomes: do you just pat your daughter on the tush and push her in the direction of the kindergarten door or do you prolong the painful goodbye until she's ready to leave you?

The answer: You leave! And fast! In fact, run! Because **if you don't leave, they won't leave**, and if they won't leave, then you've got yourself a problem with potentially ugly consequences. And you can only imagine what that must look like. It's not pretty. Believe me; I've seen it up close. It involves crying and flailing and kicking and screaming. And that's just with the parents.

After years and years in a kindergarten classroom and elementary school front office, you can bet that I've seen some pretty dicey drop-off disasters—everything ranging from crying moms and shrieking kids to full-on floor-slamming meltdowns and door-grabbing tantrums. I've seen both the ugly and the nasty. I've watched kids bolt across the playground after their parents' car; I've seen them lock themselves in bathroom stalls; I've seen kids literally hogtie themselves to their parent's leg. Name it, and I've probably seen it.

Like the third grade girl in the classroom down the hall from mine who refused to get out of the car every morning. Monday through Friday, she held onto seatbelts or car doors as a way of avoiding going to school. And her parents were super passive about it, letting her dictate how long the tantrums would last. They let her get away with making up her own rules and did very little to discourage the behavior. There was kicking and yelling and thrashing. But most often, there was just a full body collapse that forced her dad to have to carry her, limp, into the building so that he could get to work. And, ironically, as soon as she got into the classroom, she was fine. A perfect example of why it's so important for us to lay down real expectations and then hold our kids accountable for their behavior.

Let's put it in different terms. You've tried taking a bandage off slowly, right? Hurts like hell and usually leaves a blotchy red mark. But rip it off quickly and it only stings for a second, then you're over it. Well, separating from our kids works basically the same way. The longer we drag out our goodbyes, the more painful it is to let go. And the bigger the emotional mark. For everyone.

I know it hurts. Letting go of our kids, even just a little bit, rips at our hearts. And sometimes, I'm honestly not sure who it hurts more—us or them? We'll call it a tie, for argument's sake.

Maybe you've been lucky up to now and you haven't had any separation issues. Well, consider yourself blessed, because separation anxiety typically kicks in when our kids are around seven or eight months old and can last until they're close to a year and a half. And when it kicks in, it can kick hard.

But even though you may have dodged the bullet up to now, it's probably unlikely that you'll dodge it altogether. Because as those of us with kids know, parenthood is not a straight line and things don't always happen exactly the way they tell us they will in Lamaze class. Just because certain milestones or behaviors appear more often at specific ages doesn't mean they're relegated to those ages. You'll learn pretty quickly (if you haven't already) that anything can happen at any time.

That's why we have to be as nimble as we can when we're raising our kids: because the ground is constantly shifting under our feet.

Even though *we* know we'll always come back, our kids don't. And no amount of reasoning with them in the heat of their separation anxiety free fall can convince them that we will. That's because the wiring in their little brains just isn't developed enough yet to grasp that we mean what we say. They're too overcome by big, scary nerves that take the logic out of everything.

And I can't say that I blame them for freaking out, because when you think about it, we've been their main go-to people pretty much since they were born. We fed them and cuddled them and clothed them and nurtured them, and now we're up and leaving them for *X* number of hours each day with people they don't really know. Honestly, I'd be bummed out too. So it makes perfect sense that they're funky about separating from us, especially once they're headed off to school.

We've been their security blanket all this time, and we all know how tough it is to give up our woobie. It's damn near impossible. But as you'll notice when you look around you, it can be done; otherwise, we'd be seeing an awful lot of high school kids dragging ratty-looking blankies with them all over town. So the good news is that separation anxiety is usually a pretty short-lived phenomenon. In other words, *this is a phase.* And how long we're stuck in the thick of it is pretty heavily dependent on us and how we handle ourselves as parents.

I guess you could say this is one of the first times as a mom or a dad that we really have to parent up. Remember

The Blinking Game we all played when we were kids? The one where we forced our eyes to stay open and resisted the urge to blink first at all costs? Tears would be streaming down our cheeks and our eyes would be burning, but we would refuse to give in. We got props for being tough. And when we won, we earned respect.

Well, dealing with a sad, crying kid at drop-off is the grown-up version of that game—only now we're playing against our kids. And **we can't blink first!** You get me? If we blink first, we lose all our street cred. Because if we're the first to cave, then our kids learn, in that one instant, that they can beat us. Then it's game over.

So our only job now is to convince our teary-eyed son that we're coming back at the end of the school day. And how do we do that? Simple. We reassure him, every day, that we're going to be waiting outside after school exactly where we're supposed to be. And then be there. It's that simple. Day in and day out, we're going to be in that spot, waiting. And day after day, our son is going to see that we're coming back, just like we told him we would that morning at drop-off. We call this *positive reinforcement*. And believe me: it works.

Here's one pitfall to watch out for, though: our kids learn very early on in life how to leverage our love for them to their advantage. They know exactly when squirting out a few tears will get them what they want. And they're not afraid to use this power against us every chance they get. That's why you'll often see them coincidentally start to well up *just* as you're turning to leave them at school. But as long as you stay strong and committed to the drop-off, both you and your kids will be fine.

There are certain critical crossroads we reach as parents, and the direction we choose to go dictates how bumpy the road is from that point on. Like the intersection we reach when we put our newborn down to sleep in their own room for the first time and the second we walk out the door, they start crying. Do we run back in and scoop them up or do we let them learn, a little bit at a time, how to soothe themselves? In that moment, we're at one of these junctures when we have to decide which direction to go, and our journey will change drastically depending on which direction we choose. Either we keep running back in every time our baby cries so we re-inforce that we'll always come when they cry or we resist the impulse and hold our ground. We wait five minutes and then go to them. Then we wait ten minutes. Then twenty after that. Then, all of a sudden, we have a baby who can soothe herself to sleep. BOOM!

This is the cry-it-out method Dr. Benjamin Spock rec-ommended back in the mid-1940s. His philosophy was so simple—the sooner babies learned how to self-soothe, the better off they'd be. And the better off we as parents would be, too, in the long run. And, wouldn't you know, he was right. This approach holds true today and applies to so much more than just sleeping. After all, how do you think any of us learned how to swim or walk or talk? Someone was holding on to us in the beginning and, eventually, they let go. See my point?

Ok, back to drop-off anxiety.

Why, then, can some kids just trot off to school without even needing to say goodbye to us? Well, as it happens, some kids are just born a little more anxious than others. That's all. Some are born good swimmers, some have perfect pitch, some have night terrors. Some are outgoing, while others are more conservative by nature. It's just the luck of the genetics draw. The thing is, though, as much as certain aspects of our kids' behavior is biological, a lot of it has to do with us and how we parent them. If we yell, chances are good they'll yell. If we hit, they'll hit. If we're obnoxious, our kids are most likely going to be obnoxious. And so on. So if we make an effort to be calm and rational when we're with our kids, then chances are pretty high that that's what they'll pick up on after time.

Along with maintaining a good, positive attitude around our children, there are plenty of other things that we can do to help our anxious kids to be a little more relaxed. And these things are easy and fun for both us and them.

I was a big note-writer when my kids were in school. Still am, actually. And I got it from my own mom, who was notorious for sending me sweet little just-thinking-of-you notes in my lunch when I was a kid. And I loved them because they were a way of connecting with her while I was at school and we were apart. They were also the perfect little reminder that she was thinking of me too during the day. To this day, I still write my girls notes on special occasions, like when they've got a big test or a big track meet, and even though they're reluctant to admit it sometimes, they've both fessed up that they still love it.

So it's things like hiding notes in their lunches, and making goodbyes short and sweet, and anticipating a little extra funkiness on Monday mornings that help give us a competitive edge against separation anxiety. It's being mindful of these things that makes the transition to the school routine easier on us and on our kids.

Here's a free tip: **parenting is really all about the follow-through**. It's about saying what we mean and meaning what we say. (At least the majority of the time.) And the most successful parents are almost always the ones who consistently put their money where their mouth is and follow through with things like consequences or actions or promises. The truth is, it only takes a few times digging in our heels and holding the line for our kids to realize that we mean business. And that's really all they need to know. Because whether they're conscious of it or not (and most aren't), our kids take great comfort in having limits and boundaries. It's just our job as parents to remember that it's our responsibility not only to set them but to enforce them as well.

Myth #4

Myth: My kid is making new friends now, so I'm gonna get replaced.

Reality: We'll *always* be their first best friend.

Now that our kids are in school and spending time with lots of other people, e.g., classmates and teachers and other parents, it's no surprise that we're feeling insecure. But don't worry too much, because we'll always be on our kid's short list no matter how many other people come into their lives. And from here on out, there are gonna be *a lot*. Rest assured. Fortunately for us, though, this growing-up thing happens just gradually enough that we can manage to hang on.

The fact is that kids grow up. Sorry to be a spoiler, but it's just what happens. Even though most of us would love to freeze our little pocket-sized cuties exactly the way they are right now, we can't. So our smartest move as parents is to embrace the idea that *change is good*. Because change, she's a comin'. And she's comin' fast. That's why we need to trust in the fact that every stage with our kids will be more blissful than the last. (I'm laughing out loud now.)

Parenting is a free-for-all; I don't care what anyone says. No class or book or nugget of wisdom from our own parents can prepare us for what the real reality show is like. And once our kids leave the safety and security of the BabyBjörn for the real world, all bets are off.

The only thing I can tell you for sure is that the ground will always shift under our feet just as soon as we get our bearings. Once we get used to one stage, the next one comes and knocks us off balance. That's just parenthood. And one of the biggest changes we have to accept once our kids reach school age is that they're going to have a world full of new faces rotating in and out of their lives from this point on. That's why one of the best things we can do for them, even though we all know it's not easy, is to step aside and encourage them to reach out and make new connections. And as hard as it is, it's our responsibility as parents.

We have to learn to digest the idea that we're not the only ones in our child's world anymore. And the first time that really becomes obvious to us is when we see the new array of people that our kids are interacting with on a daily basis once they start school. Even if you're homeschooling your kids, this is the time they're likely to start meeting a lot of new people through homeschool groups or any sports or extracurricular activities they get involved with. It's when they start recognizing that the world is much, much bigger than their yard or neighborhood or town. And it's intimidating, believe me.

Walking into a brand-new environment, filled with brand-new everything, usually produces two distinctly different reactions from our kids. Some of them will embrace the change and drop your hand and go, while others will grab onto your pant leg like a pit bull and hang on for dear life. And it's a crapshoot, really, in terms of which kids will react which way.

That's why the best thing we can do for our daughter who just turns and runs happily into the classroom is to turn away ourselves and leave. Just leave so they can learn to find their own way. So they can cast their own net and haul in their own catch.

And for our son who's hugging our leg, we need to pry him off and encourage him to find a friend. And if he can't, we also need to turn away and leave. Because this is that point where our kids have to start learning to rely on themselves and on other people. And we have to find a way to be OK with that.

See, even though we're so used to being joined at the hip that we'd just as soon pick him up and bring him home and try again another year, we can't. We have to start fraying the umbilical cord. We don't have to cut it altogether, but we do have to make a few shallow cuts to help our kids become more independent.

The good news is that there's *never* going to be an easier time for our kids to make new friends than in the early grades in school, as hard as that may seem when you're right in the thick of it. But it's in kindergarten and the first few years of school that there are no real party lines to worry about in terms of making friends. Boys are friends with girls just as comfortably as boys are friends with other boys, and the same goes for girls. Future jocks are friends with future nerds, and future tomboys play with future fashion designers.

That's because gender and cliques are meaningless at this age. Cooties haven't gone mainstream, and everyone's pretty androgynous. In other words, it's pretty much just a giant lovefest. But even more significant than that, *there's no drama.* So my advice to you is to enjoy the calm before the storm while you can. Because the drama storm *will* come. You remember the tornado in *The Wizard of Oz*, right?

In kindergarten, though, your daughter's biggest social issue will most likely involve her crying over actual spilt milk. Other than that, friendship conflicts at that age are relatively harmless. *That's **my** eraser top! NO! It's **my** eraser top! That's **my** juice box! NO! It's **my** juice box!* (All those little square boxes look alike.) Honestly, that's about the worst of it.

This is the stage where giving our kids advice is relatively easy. When we're talking about new friendships, all we have to say is, *You don't have to like everyone you meet. Because you won't. But you damn well have to be nice to everyone no matter what.* (The *damn well* part was just for emphasis. Let's leave that out until they hit middle school. By then, you'll need some extra shock value.)

Once our kids get to school and they're bridging new connections with teachers and aides and specialists, not to mention an entire classroom of peers, it's game on. And just like that, we're not the only people in their lives anymore. And that can kinda sting a little, so don't beat yourself up too badly if you're feeling all emotional watching them trot off into school. It's totally normal. We all feel that way on some level. And if your other mom or dad friends don't own up to feeling sad, then they're lying. (Either that or they're hollow and empty inside.)

Change is good, though. And after a while, that's what all of this comes down to.

These new relationships, though, are so critical to our children's social and emotional development because they give our kids the opportunity to interact with all different kinds of people in all new kinds of situations. And even though we're only talking about elementary school, that still represents a much bigger world than the one they've been used to up to now.

Because when you really think about what our kids are exposed to those first three or four years of their life, it pretty much involves us and our extended family. I mean, sure, there are some babysitters and daycare providers tossed into the mix in those early years, but that's a very different dynamic than the school routine five days a week.

So of course there's some truth to the idea that once our kids are old enough to develop meaningful friendships with other people, their circle ultimately widens. A lot. But this in no way means that they're replacing us, even though it feels that way the older and more independent they get. You just have to remember who your daughter's first legitimate best friend was: *it was you*. And, in many ways, you always will be.

I guess I'm saying that one of the important things to keep in mind is that we're constantly interacting with new people at every stage of life—everywhere from grade school to high school to college and throughout our professional lives. For most of us, though, that exposure to new people and our first friendships start when we hit kindergarten. That's when we're surrounded by our first real crop of new faces. And it's about this time, or at least it was with my girls, when our kids start to recognize that the world doesn't just consist of mom and dad. It's an awakening for them and a bittersweet moment for us.

People will constantly cycle in and out of their lives at different points and for different reasons, while some will stay for the duration. I mean, I can't begin to count the number of "best friends" my girls have had in their lives up to now. And, in most cases, they were sure each one of those friendships would go the distance. But the truth is that they don't. And when they don't—at any age—all we can do as their parents is reassure them that sometimes our friends will surprise us in the best ways and in the worst ways. And that everything has a way of coming around.

Just try to remember that no matter how many people come and go in our kids' lives, we're always going to be the one constant. The ones they're always going to be able to count on regardless of who else is in the picture.

Myth #5

Myth: My kid is a jerk and will never have any friends.

Reality: Learning to play nice is hard—but necessary.

Realistically speaking, playing nice can be a legitimate challenge for some kids. (Let's face it: it can be a challenge for a lot of grown-ups too.) And learning to navigate a world that's filled with all sorts of new people and new surroundings can be tricky, especially for little kids.

I mean, it's not easy to control yourself when you're a five- or six-year-old and you've just been thrown into a new and intimidating environment with a bunch of other strange five- and six-year-olds for the first time. For almost the whole day. Every day of the week. (Oh yeah, and everybody's parents are gone, too.)

In theory, that could mean a giant free-for-all for everyone, because everyone's new, everyone's at least a little apprehensive, and no one knows the routine yet. And in some cases, those first few weeks of school are a horror show for some kids. Because leaving home every day and going off to a place that doesn't look a thing like home, with all new faces and lots of different kinds of new rules, is a lot for little kids to process. A real lot. So it's no wonder some kids have trouble.

You just need to keep it together and not freak out when your daughter has trouble mingling with everyone around her. Or when her teacher tells you she's been a little antisocial. Or when she comes home from school and says she hates everyone in her class. Because it's all perfectly normal.

You've gotta trust me here: plenty of kids have trouble with the transition into school, so your kid is by no means a freak if he's fidgety or he can't keep his hands to himself or his teacher says he's having trouble sharing. It happens. And you, as the parent, have to just consistently reinforce the difference between good behavior and bad behavior and what's appropriate and what's not OK. And, eventually, it will take.

As parents sending our kids off to school each day, it can be incredibly nerve racking, worrying about them keeping their behavior in check and not annoying their teacher or the other kids around them. On some level, every parent I've ever met is either consciously or unconsciously stressed about getting a note sent home from their kid's teacher that says *I'd like to schedule a conference with you at your earliest convenience.* And while I certainly can't guarantee that you won't need to have some kind of conversation about your kid's behavior somewhere down the line, the likelihood that your kid is going to be tossed out of public school for not playing nice is low. Very, very low.

My point here is that, as the parent, you just can't get too consumed by your own nervousness about what your kids are going to do when they're temporarily out of your reach each day. You need to remember that learning how to successfully interact as a member of a class is one of the main purposes of kindergarten and these early grades. (You didn't actually think it was about learning stuff, did you?)

See, right now you're preoccupied with your kid making a good first impression when she gets to school. And that's what every one of us is preoccupied with at this point. But you've gotta stay somewhat realistic at the same time. Your kid is going to screw up. She's going to say the wrong thing or do the wrong thing or behave badly in some way, shape, or form. And usually at the most inopportune times. That's just a given. But to worry about it day in and day out is just a colossal waste of your time and energy. Babies grow up and become kids, and eventually, kids go to school. By themselves. We don't spend each day in class with them for the first half of the year while they get acclimated. We drop them off on the first day of school and we leave. And in most cases, they figure out the Dos and Don'ts before too long.

Let me put it in different terms. That mama bird in the nest in the tree outside your bedroom window is getting ready to do what every bird mama before her has done for millions of years. (What you're doing right now.) She's grown and nurtured her little bird baby since the minute he was born, and she's just crossing her wings and saying a prayer that she's given him all the knowledge and tools he needs to avoid splattering on the ground when she pushes his little bird butt out of the nest. She's given him the tools to fly on his own and start making his way with all the new little birdies who live outside the nest. And wouldn't you know it: her little bird baby flies on the first try. Just like most of our kids.

OK, so I'm obviously slightly dumbing down the process of raising our kids and teaching them how to behave and play nice when they're out on their own, but the basics are still the same.

Now a kindergarten classroom full of twenty six-year-olds is slightly different than a nest full of dove babies, but the basics are still the same. All of us, bird moms and human moms and dads alike, have spent the last five or six years devoted solely to raising our kids to be decent, kindhearted little people who'll get along with everyone and toe the line. The blunt reality is that none of our kids can be expected to toe the line one hundred percent of the time. We just have to cross our fingers and say a little prayer that they do it the majority of the time.

And that's the thing about kindergarten and those early years in school: this is the first real time in our child's life when they're supposed to start figuring stuff out for themselves. (Emphasis on the word *start*.) They're *supposed* to fall out of trees and spill off bikes and learn what it feels like to be chosen last for the dodgeball team. They're *supposed* to learn that it's not OK to poke someone in the ribs just because they can't have the green crayon. They're *supposed* to figure out that they can't always sit next to their best friend at the lunch table. They're *supposed* to learn that telling secrets about their friend while she's standing directly in front of them, looking them squarely in the face, is not OK. And more often than not, they're going to find this stuff out by doing it the wrong way first, a.k.a. learning it the hard way. So don't fall to pieces if you get a call or an email or a note from the teacher about Charlie not keeping his hands to himself. It happens. And it may happen more than once or twice. But they *will* figure it out. And what you need to do on your end is reinforce what's being taught on the school end. Because when there's consistency in the message that's being sent, it eventually gets received.

Of course, working in a classroom for over a decade, I've witnessed, firsthand, some pretty extreme cases of kids not being able to handle being in a mainstream classroom. I've seen everything from biters and hitters and pokers to kickers and spitters and pinchers and anything in between. I've listened as kids barely as high as my waist screamed swear words that would embarrass even a lifelong merchant marine. And I've watched a kid run down a hallway and rip every piece of artwork down without breaking his stride (while screaming obscenities, of course). You get my point.

But you need to remember that most of those kinds of examples are unique situations where a child has a diagnosed behavioral issue that requires either a one-on-one aide to monitor them while they're in a classroom or a different classroom setting altogether. This isn't the norm. I say again: **this isn't the norm**. Besides, if your kid's behavior is that severe that it requires intervention, then you can rest assured that someone on the administrative side is probably going to intervene.

For the majority of parents whose kids are doing typical kid stuff like squirming all over the rug during the morning meeting, not keeping their hands to themselves, and talking during read aloud, this is surprisingly normal behavior. Like the boy in my kindergarten class who just couldn't manage to keep his fingers out of his nose. The kid literally left a trail of boogers everywhere he went. And while it was disgusting to those of us who shared a classroom with him, it was totally normal behavior and very short lived. Within a matter of weeks, he gradually did it less and less because we reacted to it less and less. We told him it was inappropriate behavior and explained that no one wanted to be around him if his fingers were in his nose up to his wrist. Then we ignored it. And the ignoring it was what did the trick. Because since he wasn't getting a reaction from anyone anymore, he lost interest in doing it at all.

So when you're up at two a.m., lying in bed in a cold sweat over the fact that your daughter doesn't transition well from outdoor recess to circle time, you have to consider the fact that she's in kindergarten and that's one of the things they're there to learn.

Think of it this way—school has a giant learning curve, and our kids show up on the first day in all different locations on that curve. In the end, though, as they progress through these early grades, they figure it all out. They learn not to blurt out the answer or to interrupt. They figure out that you dot an *i* and cross a *t*. And they discover that you can't just swipe a ball out of someone's hand because you feel like playing with a ball.

The thing to keep firmly in mind is that all of these kids meshing together under one roof are coming from all different types of environments, with different rules and different expectations. Some kids are coming at all this as only children (like I did) or as the older sibling or the middle brother or the younger sister. Some are coming from homes with one dad and no mom or two dads or one mom and no dad (also like me). And as all these little guys migrate from life under their family's roof to the brave new world of school, they have roughly zero transition time. The problem is that it takes time to figure out what behavior is acceptable and what behavior just won't fly. It takes time to figure out that you can't talk to your classmates at school in the same way that you do to your brother in the privacy of your shared bedroom.

Accept the fact that our kids come home with a new best friend pretty much on a daily basis. So get used to them being best friends or worst enemies with someone they met that day at recess. Friendship at this age is like a revolving door. On Monday and Tuesday, Jack is going to be your son's best friend, but by Wednesday afternoon, they're going to hate each other. That's just how it happens most of the time, but knowing it's coming ahead of time will allow you to take it all in stride. And that's because our kids haven't got a clue yet what friendship really means. They're flying blind without any navigation instruments. And that's why they keep crashing and burning every time they take off again with someone new. But eventually, over time, they get a feel for what they're doing and their friendships are built on more than just a mutual love of Star Wars Legos.

It's the same way with competition at that age. When most young kids are put in a competitive situation, they're trying to win. Because at that age, to them, games and competition are mostly black and white. They're about winning and losing and not much else. And that's because they're little kids who are just starting to learn that there's so much more to competition than winning and losing. But when they're just starting out, the sportsmanship aspect or the being-part-of-a-team piece or the confidence-building part are just too much for many of them to grasp early on. So that's why we tend to see a healthy amount of fits and temper flare-ups when they're at recess or in gym class or on their first youth soccer team.

So if you're getting back comments in their first progress report like *Needs Improvement* under the *Demonstrates Self-Control* category or *Unsatisfactory* in the *Plays Well with Others* column, don't immediately start filling out applications for boarding school. Because plenty of kids struggle with these social skills in the beginning.

Just try not to stress too much about how your kids are interacting with people at this age, especially with their peers. Because they're going to screw up, make mistakes, and embarrass themselves (and you) on a regular basis. That's a guarantee. Which is why you need to keep things in perspective and remember that, at this point, they've been alive for fewer years than you have fingers on both hands. Or less. So expecting them to have perfect manners and behavior and people skills right out of the womb just isn't realistic. These things are all learned—learned from us and their teachers and the world around them. But it takes time. In some cases, even a lifetime. (I know plenty of adults who still haven't gotten it yet.)

We eventually learned how to play nice and so will they. So just keep reinforcing the good behavior and calling them out on the bad stuff, and sooner than later, it will all click. Ultimately, the kicking and shoving and biting and hair-pulling will stop. And while I know, at this point in the game, you're seeing no end in sight, my now-adult kids and all their former menace friends are living, breathing proof that I speak the truth. Just hang on. Because like all nauseating and traumatizing amusement park rides you've ever been on, they do eventually level out. Just like this joyride will. I promise.

Myth #6

Myth: If I punish my kid, she'll hate me.

Reality: Kids need consequences and boundaries.

Kids break rules. It's just what they do. They're wired for it. Hell, it's what *we* all did when we were kids. And it's our job as their parents to break them all like little wild horses—a job that takes endless amounts of time, incredible dedication, and a ton of patience. But it *can* be done. I swear. I've personally done it twice, so I've got at least a few handy nuggets of wisdom I can toss your way.

One way or another, every kid tests limits and pushes boundaries and tries our patience. I guess you could say it's like a rite of passage. Because a big part of growing up as a kid involves figuring out what you *can* and *can't* get away with. And we only need to look as far back as our own childhood for proof that we all do it to one degree or another.

I mean, how many times did you or your sister or brother push your mom's buttons? Too many to count, I'm sure. And how many times did we get busted by our dad for blowing our curfew even though we knew we'd get reamed if we were even three minutes late? Plenty. And how often did we watch our friends make the dumbest decisions—like ski jumping off the roof of the house—in spite of the fact that they knew it would end badly? Too often, believe it or not.

These things—and *so* many more—happen because kids are immature. Even though I was a pretty good kid growing up, in terms of following rules, I still did my share of thoughtless, irresponsible things even after my parents gave me pretty clear-cut warnings not to. Things like scooting down a handicapped ramp on my little plastic scooter immediately after my mom said *Do **not** ride anywhere near that ramp, because you'll go too fast and won't be able to stop.* Which I ignored, of course. Because, like most little kids, I assumed I was invincible. In my underdeveloped little brain, it never occurred to me that I could lose control and end up flying over the handlebars, landing in a full face-plant on the concrete (chin first). Twelve stitches later . . .

Or, a year later, when my mom asked me to walk cautiously around the stray, historically unfriendly dog in my neighborhood to avoid getting bitten. Which my naive little intellect translated as code for *sneak behind him and pull his tail.* More stitches. My poor mom. That poor dog.

Or when my daughter Libby decided to momentarily become a door-slammer, even though I was *very* clear about what would happen if people slammed doors. She was testing limits, obviously, trying to annoy me because I denied another request to go to the mall. So she let the door fly. To which I issued an ultimatum. *Slam it again, and you'll wish you didn't.* You can guess what happened. Needless to say, a flathead screwdriver was all I needed to make my point. Her door lived in the garage for three days. No doors have been slammed since.

I guess what I'm trying to say is that our kids will challenge our authority and our rules and our advice every single chance they get. And they do that for what feels like a really, really long time. Long enough that you're almost convinced that they'll never outgrow the behavior. In their defense, though, the reason why kids constantly do and say dumb stuff and have to be disciplined is because they haven't been around long enough to understand the rules of *cause* and *effect.* Which is why they're constantly making the same mistakes over and over and over again. To the point when, as the mom and dad, you just want to bash your head against a wall because they never seem to learn the lesson. But don't panic if you're feeling that way. First of all, we all feel that way at some point along the line. And second, they *do* eventually stop. That's because it takes a long, long time for a child's brain to form all the connections necessary to learn how to reason and think like a rational, semi-intelligent person.

Now, I try never to get too technical, but sometimes, it serves a purpose. By understanding *why* something functions the way it does, it usually helps us to better know how to manage it (or, in our case, how to manage *them*). If we have at least a decent idea of what's going on under the hood, we can better handle ourselves when there's a breakdown. Perfect example: our kids.

So with that in mind, the scientific explanation for what's going on in your kid's head when they're young and making the same mistakes every four minutes has to do with synapses. In simple terms, synapses are links between two nerve cells comprising a tiny gap across which impulses pass by diffusion of a neurotransmitter. (I know; I've already gotten too technical. But stay with me.) In English, and very crudely put, synapses help transmit messages around our brains by sending electrical impulses from one neuron to the next, to the next, and so on. Fascinating stuff, actually. And broken down even further, so that the average parent can understand: Your kids will keep flipping a nutty over the same stupid stuff until the right connections are made in their little brains. Which will ultimately allow them to stop.[5]

The thing is, the connections get stronger the more our kids use them. In other words, they have to keep screwing up until they learn not to screw up anymore. And that means they don't often figure stuff out on the first try. Or the second. Or the thirtieth.

A lot like how muscle tissue develops, actually. We can't build muscle overnight. It's a process. We lift weights, we rest, our muscle fibers break down and then regenerate, and, little by little, over time, we get stronger. And the same exact process happens when we try to teach our kids how to behave. They make a bad choice, we discipline them or give them a consequence, and, little by little, they learn and remember what will happen to them if they pull the same stunt again. In other words, we're strengthening their character rather than their muscle. Get it?

The good thing is, most of the stuff our kids get into when they're young is, like my husband likes to say, pretty vanilla. It's more or less harmless. Annoying, but harmless.

In the early years, kids are just too inexperienced at life to realize that when they do or say something that's inappropriate, they're going to get nailed for it by someone. At least most of the time. That, my friends, is where we step in.

As new human beings, they simply haven't developed the cognitive power to see two seconds beyond where they are at the moment. That means when they push our buttons or make bad decisions, chances are excellent that they haven't even bothered to think past their words hitting the air. This is that critical point where we have to put our money where our mouth is and hand out consequences. Little ones for the little stuff and bigger ones for the bigger stuff. Although, between us, **it's not really as much *what* the consequence is—it's that there *is* one.** Which means that the real key to effectively disciplining our kids is disciplining them at all with some kind of consistency.

It's never easy to discipline our kids. No parent wants to bring down the hammer, believe me. God knows I didn't. But it is necessary, both for our kids' well-being and for ours. That's because kids need boundaries—clear-cut, defined boundaries—that help them differentiate right from wrong.

It's that simple. And setting those boundaries is entirely our responsibility.

Think of it another way. What would happen to the new dog you just brought home from the shelter if you let him out in the backyard and the yard didn't have a fence? Bye-bye, doggy. The dog can't be expected to set its own boundaries. Dogs don't do that. And neither do our kids.

Most of the heavy lifting we do as moms and dads is really just about common sense and backbone. Unfortunately, not all parents are born with equal parts common sense and spine, both of which go hand in hand when raising kids.

See, whether you're thinking about it this way or not, the truth is, **we're all products of who and where we come from**. At least to some degree. So that means that who our kids become as people is a direct result of how we handle them as kids.

Now I know this seems like an obvious concept, and you're probably wondering why I'm even bothering to bring it up. Well, it just so happens that there are way more parents out there than you even realize who give their kids ultimatums and threaten consequences for bad decisions or behavior and then don't follow through at the eleventh hour.

Parents blurt out that TV privileges will be taken away or electronics will be forfeited as a consequence, and then they cave once they have to follow through. Everyone hates to be the bad cop when it comes to disciplining our kids. Believe me: I get it. I've been the bad and the good cop, and they're both tricky. Because when you're the bad guy a few times, the perception of you becomes that you *are* the bad guy. And no parent wants to be typecast as the mean one. But then if you're the good guy all the time, your kids will steamroll you. Happens every time. They'll play on your sensitivity and what they perceive as your softheartedness, and they'll kick you in the crotch every time.

I see it daily working in a school. I see kids habitually forgetting backpacks and homework and textbooks and backpacks (Yeah, amazing, isn't it?) and parents coming in and swearing up and down that it's the last time they'll bail out their kid. Week in and week out, these same parents will storm into school angry and frustrated at their kids for forgetting things, yet they never give their daughter the obvious consequence of doing without whatever it was that she forgot. It drives me absolutely nuts.

One mom would actually time her drop-off visits to coincide with when her son's class would be transitioning from the classroom to music or gym or recess. She knew his schedule well enough that she managed to walk into the front lobby at the *exact* time her kid was coming down the hall. It was uncanny, almost like she had some cosmic GPS tracking sensor telling her his exact location. And even though she'd always complain to me that he'd forget his head if it wasn't attached, she'd still bring his sneakers or science binder or lunchbox every single time. Every. Single. Time. And the kid knew it, so there was never a reason for him to take ownership or responsibility. Classic enabling right there.

Sure, as a kindergartener or a first or second grader, our kids haven't been exposed to enough of the school routine yet to remember everything, so we cut them some slack until they get into a groove, usually around third or fourth grade. But the overarching rule is still true, even for these little guys, that if they're misbehaving or not following directions, there needs to be a consequence. In school. At home. Everywhere.

OK, so even though the word *consequence* usually has a negative connotation, it doesn't always have to be a bad thing. It's like anything; it depends on how you spin it. That's why your goal as a parent shouldn't be to prevent negative behavior (that's just a lost cause); it should actually be to reinforce positive behavior.

Which is why we should never be giving our kids **punishments** for their behavior. That's nothing but negative, especially when you consider that a punishment is nothing more than retribution or getting back at someone. And we both know that's no way to raise a kid. A **consequence**, though, is an effect or result of someone's actions. It's super important to understand the difference.

What we need to be doing, though, in terms of effectively disciplining our kids boils down to one thing. (OK, maybe two.) We have to consistently bring down the hammer when our kids need a consequence. And we have to **Hold the line!** at all costs. Which means that we have to use the old Yul Brynner line from *The Ten Commandments*: "So let it be written; so let it be done." Once we say it, we have to follow through with it. In fact, that's the only rule that really matters in the end. Because if we don't stand our ground, the enemy (our kids) will breach our defenses. And if our defenses are compromised, we've just lost the war.

I had one of those "battles" years ago when my youngest was around eight. We had taken a road trip to New York City to visit the American Girl store. It was a dream come true for her, and she'd waited weeks to make the trip. She had brought all of her most favorite American Girl dolls with her, dressed in their best outfits and loaded with every accessory they could carry. To her, it was like the equivalent of going to Disney World. Needless to say, I think we were somewhere around Times Square when her meltdown started. And even though I honestly can't remember the exact reason why she lost it, I do remember that it was bad. Like, really bad. So bad that Dave and I had to bring out the big guns, leaving us no choice but to issue an ultimatum. *Pull yourself together or we're not going to the American Girl store.*

Well, let's just say it didn't end well. She couldn't get a grip on herself, and so it left us no choice. She forced our hand, so we had to nix going to the American Girl store or look like the softest parents on the planet. It was brutal on everyone, but it had to be done in the interests of follow-through. We considered it a teachable moment, a life lesson. And it clearly worked, because the impact of us walking past the store and not going in was profound. Libby was devastated. (And so was I. Pretty sure I cried myself to sleep that night in the hotel.) But in the end, even though holding that line was beyond tough, it sent a necessary message that bad behavior wouldn't be tolerated without consequences. And she heard us loud and clear. So the next time she pushed our buttons and put us in a similar situation, we reminded her of that day in New York and the memory hit her hard, right between the eyes. Hard enough to derail another outburst.

So just take a series of deep breaths and resign yourself to doling out and enforcing whatever appropriate consequence is necessary in the moment. Because in this game, you need to be in it to win it.

Myth #7

Myth: My kid will never grow out of this Jekyll-and-Hyde phase.

Reality: Our kids become decent people eventually, regardless of how they start out.

I t's true what you've heard about our kids being a lot like Jekyll and Hyde. Because they are. Especially when they're young.

They flip from one mood to another to another to another with the fluidity of a synchronized swimmer, usually without even taking a breath. And it can be hard to take as the parent trying to keep up.

Even the most mild-mannered kids have their moments. And that's because as they grow into their adolescent years, start to wrestle with puberty, and struggle with all sorts of new relationships, our kids develop what seems like four hundred different personalities all rolled into one tiny body.

They're sweethearts and savages, lunatics and pussycats, all smooshed into one little kid. And this Multiple-Personality Syndrome, as I like to call it, lasts a while. Sometimes it lasts through the grammar school years and then peaks in middle school, and sometimes it follows our kids straight through grade school all the way to high school. Depends on the kid, really. But the one thing we have to remember—even when it seems like they'll never evolve—is that they do, eventually, settle into a groove. They do, eventually, come into their own.

So my suggestion to you at this point is to find a comfy seat, buckle in tight—like airplane tight—and hang on. Because this is where things start to roll upside down. But they will roll back. I promise. Because that's exactly how life was in our house when our girls both hit grade school.

Now, granted, our daughters are three years apart, so we were almost always guaranteed to have one stable kid and one lunatic at the same time. Never two of each simultaneously. And then, of course, it almost always flip-flopped once one of them hit solid ground. Then the other one went nuts. But that's just par for the course with kids.

As soon as we get even the slightest grip on where their heads are at, the ground shifts under our feet and we fall into a big, ugly sinkhole. A sinkhole that we never saw coming. Then we climb out and repeat. Over and over and over again.

A great example is how our youngest, Libby, started out as the most even-keeled kid, never really swinging too high or too low, and then slowly morphed into a pretween who was happy one minute and (literally) unhinged the next. She went from being unflappable most of the time to slamming doors and acting snarky and pushing everyone's buttons. God forbid when one of us asked her to clean her room. Not a good scene.

She went through a phase—a very long phase—where she wore just about everything she was feeling draped all over her like a patchwork quilt. And it was challenging to be around because nothing Dave or I said did very much to defuse her crazier moments.

To be honest, the only thing that really helped was time. And that's what I've come to learn is the real, true equalizer. Because our kids don't realize how unreasonable and ridiculous they're acting just because we point it out to them. In fact, pointing it out to them is almost always a bad move. They almost always have to become self-aware on their own. And that takes time.

The irony is that now, close to a decade later, Libby's settled back into that easygoing girl. Her personality ebbed and flowed through lots of different versions of the same original kid and ultimately came back around to the basic personality she started with. Because that's who she always was at heart. And that's what tends to happen when kids grow up and mature (key word is *mature*).

I used to see it in my kindergarten and elementary classrooms all the time: these sweet little girls would play beautifully for ninety percent of recess and then someone would snap because their piece of sidewalk chalk broke in half. Whether it's someone flipping a switch and melting down because they don't want to share the jump rope or someone grabbing a fistful of someone else's hair because they want a turn on the

monkey bars, these sudden and extreme changes in temperament are everywhere when you're dealing with young kids.

Boys sobbing in the corner of the playground because the
other team won't give them another swing at bat. Or girls
being overdramatic and reduced to tears because they aren't
allowed to join the four square game. It's everywhere, and it's
normal. Albeit annoying and ridiculous, but normal. And
that's what we have to keep in mind.

Until they grow up and develop what will eventually be
their adult personality, our kids are sampling tons of different
behaviors and traits until they find the ones they like best. It's
kind of like window shopping—only the world is their window and they're totally creeping on everyone around them.
Actually, what they're really doing is just quietly observing.
And most of the time, they're doing it subconsciously.

And the journey through all of these different personalities
can be a hairy one because some of the things they pick up will
seem an awful lot like they're trying to jam a round peg into a
square hole. The truth is, a lot of the things they end up saying
and doing seem like a real departure from the stuff we're used
to seeing and hearing. Because the point is, at this age, our
kids simply lack the capacity to keep themselves in check a lot
of the time.

Like when Riley, my oldest, and her friend Alex decided it
would be funny to lock all the parents out of Alex's house when
they were in preschool. Incredibly stupid decision. Totally not
cool. And certainly not something we thought they'd ever do.

They were having a playdate and they were having fun, so
they weren't ready to say goodbye quite yet. (Typical of most
good playdates.) But it was getting late, and we needed to get

home for dinner, so we gave the kids the five-minute warning and headed outside to chat on the front porch. Unbeknownst to us, though, the kids snuck downstairs and locked the front door without us knowing. Needless to say, the looks on our faces must've been classic when we tried the doorknob and realized we were locked out. And of course, they ran and hid in the playroom, way up in the loft upstairs, so they couldn't even hear us yelling to them to unlock the door. Totally out of character for both of them. But that's just the stuff kids do when they're young. They push buttons and test limits and act on raw impulse.

Eventually, the kids came downstairs and we persuaded them to open the door. And both of them knew instantly that they had crossed a line into a dark place of disobedience. Which they picked up on the second we walked back through the door and they saw our faces. And that was punishment enough because our fear and annoyance scared the crap out of them. So as most parents do when we rescue our kids from a potentially dangerous situation, we focused more on the fact that they were safe and sound and hadn't lit the house on fire than on their bonehead move of locking us out of the house. No real harm, no real foul.

Now, I don't want you to worry too much, because that's all normal. I say again: **that's totally normal**. It's what kids do. They watch everything and everyone around them, consciously and unconsciously deciding what qualities they like best. So at this point, it's a waste of time and energy for us to try and gauge which traits they're going to hang onto. It's almost pointless to try and figure out who our kid is on the inside yet because they don't even know themselves. That's why it's so important that we encourage our kids to "try on" a whole bunch of different hats, so to speak. This is the time in their life when it's OK to jump from a season of soccer to a season of field hockey to a season of pottery to a season of guitar lessons. As long as they respect the commitment they make to the club or the team or the class, they should reserve the right to decide if it's for them or not. Because unless they experiment with the options around them, they're never going to know what fits.

Let me put it like this: kids are like chameleons—they're constantly changing their behavior to blend into their surroundings. You know, snarky is as snarky does. (And if you don't know yet, you will.) It's only when they're older, like in high school and beyond, that they start to level off and gravitate toward the more mature traits like patience, humility, gratitude, and respect, to name a few of the most popular ones. (Some of my favorites, anyway.)

You've seen it (or you will), when your daughter comes home from a playdate with a girl who has, shall we say, a different code of conduct in her family. Like maybe she's allowed to be a little bossy or she's a little spoiled or maybe a little fresh. And then, all of a sudden, you're sitting around the dinner table with your daughter and she barks at you to get up and get her some more milk. And you're like, *Wait, what?!*

Because when they're young, our kids are stimulated and influenced in so many different ways and by so many people that it's impossible for them to pick and choose which traits suit them best. It's like being in a penny candy store with eight thousand pennies—so much to choose from. (At least in the beginning, when they're young. I know that's how it was for my own kids. They go from being these cuddly little smoosh balls who hang on our every word to these rabidly insane freaks who won't let you open the car door to drop them off at school unless the radio is off. It's nuts.)

Even though our kids are born with a very distinct natural predisposition that's unique to just them, they're constantly sampling different personas and attitudes to see which ones they like best. Sometimes deliberately and sometimes not. Sometimes good ones and sometimes not. Unfortunately for us, though, we get to be the ones who deal with the fallout from all that dabbling. We're the ones who endure all their manic mood swings and hysteria because they're forever shifting from one personality to another.

And to be quite honest, it can be a huge pain in the butt. Because if your kids are anything like mine, they're one way in the house, one way at school, one way with family, and one way with the gen pop when they're in the outside world. And it's exhausting. I mean, who of us hasn't had our kid say something totally rude to our face in the privacy of our car or our living room that they'd never dare say in front of another adult? Right? But they act like that because they just don't know what to do with all those personalities they've got jammed inside them.

Remember, aside from their genetic code and some hereditary tendencies and traits, kids come out of the womb pretty much a clean slate—like an empty bowl waiting for ingredients. And every interaction they have, every word they hear, from the second they're born, all blend together, almost like cookie dough. Ultimately, they form something sweet and irresistible.

My oldest daughter, Riley, now in college, was super cautious and reserved when she was little. She always stayed squarely inside her comfort zone with things like sports and school and never aggressively pushed herself beyond what she thought were her limits. She did things at her own pace and never let herself be influenced by what other kids around her were doing.

Skip ahead a little to when she got to high school and mix in all the new people and experiences that she was exposed to, and everything changed. She morphed into this fearless, inspired, confident, passionate woman. She was driven to experience everything she could and did it at her full capacity. She was motivated by the people around her, which is exactly when she learned how to finally push beyond her limits. (See, it does happen.) But it took time.

And that's the thing about parenting . . . we can't seem to imagine our kids evolving out of the phase they're in right now. But they do. We can't imagine that one day they'll be able to walk on their own and eat on their own and drive on their own. But it happens. And they pick up a lot of cool traits along the way.

See, even though we're all born with very unique temperaments and personalities, our DNA is our DNA no matter what. Some of our kids are born with a sense of humor, some without. Some with the ability to empathize and sympathize. Some with an almost freakish self-confidence. And some without.

Now, sure, we can get a pretty decent sense early on whether or not we've got a high-strung kid or a strong-willed kid or a competitive kid. Those qualities are usually pretty obvious from early in the game and generally stay embedded in their personality for the long haul. But it's the stuff that's mixed in with those traits, like the qualities they pick up from the people around them—most notably us—that can have the biggest impact on our kids' overall personalities. Remember, guys, we're the single most influential people in our child's life. We help shape and mold who they become not only by what we say but, even more importantly, by what we do.

For instance, if we're a type A personality and have the tendency to be high strung or super intense, some of that is likely to rub off on our kids. It's kind of inevitable. Like if we're a yeller or we discipline by hitting, then we shouldn't be all that surprised if we raise a yeller or a hitter of our own.

So I guess what I'm really trying to say here is that even though our kids are born products of their genetic codes, they're also mostly blank canvases with nothing more than a basic background. And for each of them, that canvas absorbs new mediums in very different ways. Some things they're exposed to will be permanent, while others will bead up and drip off over time.

It's our job to supply the paint and the studio. Oh yeah, and the turpentine for cleaning up the ginormous mess they make along the way.

Myth #8

Myth: Drama is a middle school and high school problem.

Reality: There's no way around it: kids equal drama.

rama. Just the single, stand-alone word is enough to make any parent vomit in their mouth. (It's almost as traumatic as the word *lice*. Almost.)

Because drama can pop up at any time, without any warning, without any real rhyme or reason, and it can be debilitating, sucking the life out of us and out of our kids. Not to mention that it's often tricky to resolve. So it's important, as a parent, to be able to keep it all in perspective so we ensure that our kids can do the same.

See, it doesn't matter how well adjusted or easygoing our kids are; drama happens. It just does. And it doesn't discriminate either. It affects everyone, regardless of their social status or gender or age. How we address it and how we teach our kids to deal with it, though, can make all the difference in terms of everyone surviving it.

As far as the kinds of drama we're likely to see at this age, we're mainly talking about two categories. You've got your **friend drama** and your **home drama**, two decidedly different varieties. But both can be dicey.

Broken down into simplest terms, friend drama involves any kind of conflict our kids have with other kids. (But you knew that.) It includes, but isn't limited to, stuff like teasing and bullying and being excluded. And it can come from the most unlikely places, like the kids we'd never expect. You know, the ones who were our daughter's best friend two days ago. Which is exactly why we've always told our own kids that people will surprise them in the *best* and in the *worst* of ways.

So as our kids start experiencing drama out in the real world, we need to constantly reinforce the fact that everyone is dealing with emotional growing pains but not everyone deals with them the same way. Kids are impressionable. We all know that. Some more than others. And a lot of kids get sucked into the world of drama because it gives them a feeling of being in control and they're just not mature enough yet to know that ninety-nine percent of it is a ridiculous waste of time and energy. For them, it's a way to assert themselves and have power over other kids, wrong as that may be. Though they do tend to grow out of it in time. (Just usually not soon enough for us.)

I've seen kindergarteners bring other kindergarteners to tears over everything from what they're wearing to how they smell (yeah, it happened) to how they throw a ball to whether or not they like tuna sandwiches (my youngest daughter got that one). And then, by the time they've grown up a little and matured and realized that saying mean stuff is actually hurtful, they knock it off and everyone is friends again. (At least most of the time.)

In contrast, home drama is a whoooooole different animal. Fortunately for us, our kids reserve their worst behavior for home. No matter what kind of kid you're raising, no matter how in control and well adjusted they are, at some point, they all melt down in the privacy of their own home. And once that happens, the drama oozes out like an open head wound. It's like they say: *We never truly see our own child the way they rest of the world sees them.* Which I can confirm from experience is one hundred percent true.

A perfect example are the kids I see coming through the front doors at school who would never dare open their mouth to me or their teachers but wouldn't hesitate to mouth off to their mom over something stupid like packing them room-temperature Gatorade in their lunchbox. (I've seen it. It happened.) And as horrifying as it is to watch as a bystander, it's like Bruce Lee's one-inch punch to the chest when you're that parent and the blows are flying. The reason, though, is because our kids feel a very different comfort level with family, under their own roof, than they do with the general population.

This particular Gatorade girl was a piece of work. She was an only child, and her mom was totally devoted to catering to her daughter's every ridiculous whim. If the daughter was carrying her backpack and had to use another hand to carry a project or a lunchbox, she'd refuse, telling mom to carry it to class for her. And she wouldn't hesitate to lash out at mom if other people were around. Didn't matter if a teacher was standing in front of her or the principal or the guidance counselor; she'd let the demands fly. Freely. And even though most kids reserve their really epically bad behavior for us, in the privacy and comfort of home, there are plenty of kids out there who don't think twice about behaving badly or being rude or disrespectful in public.

Let me tell you, though, that how we handle those outbursts and demands can make us or break us. If we allow that kind of behavior, then we're enablers. We're to blame for having dramatic, insolent kids. Because if they're talking to *us* like that, publicly, just imagine what they're saying to their friends and how they're behaving with their teachers and other parents. That's why we need to make sure that we set a clear expectation with our kids early on so they know that kind of behavior won't be tolerated. Which is exactly what Dave and I tried to do from the get-go. Our kids knew that if they crossed a certain line (like talking back to us in public or throwing a fit because we wouldn't let them have something), then they weren't going to see the light of day for a very long time. And even though that strategy wasn't always guaranteed, enough reinforcement of that idea over the years helped instill a healthy fear in our girls that they needed to behave respectfully. It made enough of an impression, in fact, that whenever they'd see a child grossly misbehaving out in public, they'd be horrified by the behavior and point it out to us.

Now I know most young parents don't even consider drama a viable issue until their kids hit middle school, and

Also, since most drama is so irrational and spontaneous to begin with, there's no foolproof way of dealing with it when it happens. Sorry, but that's the reality. It's actually a lot like dealing with a trick birthday candle that keeps relighting— we're never really able to snuff it out. Which is why it's our job as the moms and dads to douse the drama with a firehose if we see it's going too far. But not right away. Jumping in and getting involved when our kids are in conflict with a friend should be our last resort. Before we go for the assist, we need to back away and let them try to handle the situation on their own. Then, if the drama or bullying gets physical or they get threatened or make a threat, we move in. And fast. Because they're still naïve kids who need our guidance.

Also, and equally as important, we need to be honest with our kids and point out when *they're* actually the problem. Because as we all know, there are always two sides to every story, and as much as we'd love to assume that our kids are always angels, they're not. They're human and they make mistakes and say and do things that they shouldn't, in spite of the best upbringing and guidance.

Sometimes, though, the best thing we can do to help our kids navigate these incidents is to encourage them to stay calm, take a step back, and remind them that we're there for them when they need us. Because they're way more likely to think rationally when we're rational.

Now, since I have two girls, I don't speak boy. Not a single word. Even our dog is a girl. So I can't really talk too much about the boy side. I can really only speak to what I saw when I worked with boys every day in the classroom. And from what I've seen over the years, boy confrontations are decidedly different from girl conflicts, even though both are still emotionally draining, time consuming, and generally annoying just the same. Boys tend to bottle stuff up and get more physical, while girls tend to be a little drippier with their emotions and play more head games with each other, but both kinds have their own challenges.

Like when a bunch of boys are playing what's *supposed* to be flag football and then some kid goes rogue and flying body-slams the guy who's got the ball. Happens all the time. Then punches get thrown and someone inevitably ends up in the nurse's office with a bloody nose. Garden-variety boy drama.

Girls, though, are a different breed altogether. Our brand of drama is usually more psychologically based as opposed to physical. We get in each other's heads and then destroy each other from the inside out. And it starts early.

I mean, since I'm being totally honest here, girl drama is absolutely brutal because they mess with each other's heads. Even when they're in the younger grades. I don't know how, but they do. There's the whole crying piece that doesn't happen nearly as often with boys, and the jealousy factor, and the exaggeration factor, which all adds up to an ugly, snotty mess.

So as far as girl drama is concerned, I can probably tell you everything you ever wanted to know, but to sum it up, it sucks. That's just the plain and simple truth. Girls are dramatic by nature, so their responses to emotional situations are almost always going to be amplified.

I mean, boys can be angry at each other one minute and playing Transformers in the dirt the next. But girls—we tend to hang onto our emotions. Almost feeding off them.

On a daily basis, I'd take a group of kindergarten girls out to recess, and one minute they'd be all lovey-dovey, playing four square and braiding each other's hair, and then, without any warning at all, one of them would collapse into tears. And most of the time, it was because her friend said they couldn't sit together anymore at lunch. Devastating. Or when a bunch of second graders would talk about after-school playdate plans but one of them wasn't invited. Never a good outcome there. Or when our daughter's new BFF (you know, since yesterday's soccer practice) decides to be someone else's bestie, and the trauma is almost too intense to bear.

And these little episodes would oftentimes drag out. For what seemed like forever. Because girls like to drag stuff out and regurgitate the agony and the suffering and the crisis over and over and over until everyone in the vicinity knows about it and lines have been drawn and sides have been taken. And any girl knows this to be true. Think of girl drama like a carnival mirror that brutally distorts the real image that it's reflecting. That's girl drama: horribly distorted most of the time.

Which is the unfortunate thing about drama: so much of it centers around a power struggle. There's almost always that *one boy* or that *one girl* who just dominates everyone else. You know, the Alpha Male and the Alpha Female. We have them in all areas of our life, but the first time we're usually exposed to them is when we're young and in school. I mean, God knows I still remember the girl who bullied me through elementary school. Vividly. And that kind of drama stays with you. That stuff is toxic.

I know we've covered a lot of ground here, so now you should have the basic gist of what lies ahead. (Be glad at this point that it's too early for us to be talking about dating or social media, because that's a level of drama beyond anything you could imagine.) And you should also have a sense of how to handle drama when it happens. You'll play it exactly like you would when your toddler falls off her scooter—you won't flinch until she does. You'll stay calm and not pounce on them, hysterical and overcome by the sight of a skinned elbow. You won't react until you see how *she reacts*. And then, if the trauma is *so* bad that you have to rush over, you'll help calm her down, throw a bandage on her arm, and take her for ice cream until she forgets about it altogether. But you certainly won't perpetuate the ordeal by taking and posting pictures of the goriness on Facebook or Instagram so the whole world gets to feed into the drama, because that would be stupid. Right? Right.

It's almost like we have to consider ourselves deputized members of a bomb squad, defusing every potential explosion *before* it happens. And since we can't cut the right wire every single time, we do have to expect that some dramatic moments will inevitably blow up in our faces. Like when our daughter is amped up because her BFF didn't share her Cheese Nips at school and you try to explain that she really doesn't have to because it's *her* snack. Sometimes our explanation, as logical as it is, is useless.

So here's what we do . . . we keep as calm and as rock steady as we can when our kids are being dramatic so that we don't fan the fire. Because what happens to a fire when we fan it? It gets all the extra oxygen it needs to grow big and hostile and unruly. That's why we douse it with water instead. And, in this case, our calm, zen-like attitude is like a big sloshy bucket of water.

Myth #9

Myth: We're all speaking the same language.

Reality: We may be speaking the same language, but we don't all hear the same things.

I s anyone listening to me? Because I know words are coming out of my mouth. I can hear them. And so can everyone else around us . . . except you. Come on!

I think this pretty much sums up how most of us feel when we try to communicate with our kids. At least the majority of the time. We parents do all the talking, we make all the requests, we toss out all the directions, and our kids selectively pick and choose which things they want to respond to and when. It's called **selective hearing**. And it's real. Very, very real.

And while this selective hearing condition doesn't really fully kick in until our kids are around middle school age, it most definitely shows itself once our kids start feeling a little independent, like once they start heading off to school. Because once they realize they're old enough to be out on their own a little (even if that just means being in a supervised classroom for a few hours a day), they fancy themselves ready to take on the world. Almost instinctively, they start thinking they don't need to hear what we have to say anymore. And that becomes a bit of a problem when we're the ones trying to talk to them.

Ever hear the expression *falling on deaf ears*? Well, after raising two kids, I can definitely say that there's no doubt in my mind that that phrase was coined by a frustrated parent. Probably some mom who'd been yelling at her son through the kitchen window to come inside for dinner but the kid never came—in spite of the fact that he was looking directly at her while she was yelling at him.

See, once our kids figure out that they can *pretend* to ignore us, they gain a little bit of an upper hand. Or at least they think they do. Because, at any given time, our kids can *claim* that they just never heard us. And it's brutal because we, as the parents, can't argue that too much unless we happen to be standing directly in front of them, eyes locked, screaming their name. It's maddening, and it only gets worse.

But this condition of selective hearing is something that all of us have to deal with, at least a good chunk of the time, while our kids are young.

I've always found it hysterical that my kids could hear me talking to Dave about an ice cream craving from across the house while inside their bedroom with the door closed and earbuds in their ears. But yell to them from across the living room, eight feet away, to please get their damn backpack off the kitchen floor, and all I'd get were crickets. Nothing. No response.

I know we all have these goals when we're starting out as parents to artfully craft, uh, I mean raise, these well-behaved, model little citizens who come when we call them, never talk back, and vacuum their rooms on a regular basis without being asked. It's every parent's dream. But it's a pipe dream. Sorry. The reality is that kids ignore their parents. It's the natural order of things.

And that's what we need to remember. This is typical kid behavior, along with a boatload of other lovely behaviors, like sassing us and disrespecting us and lying to us, among a thousand others. Because even though none of us ever wants to see any of this from our own kids, we inevitably do.

I've had my own kids ignore me when I'm literally asking for a one-word answer. I've watched them respond to another parent or their teachers while they were totally ignoring me. And even though the communication breakdown happens gradually at this age, it still happens. And it still causes friction between us and our kids.

As far as I'm concerned, Charles Shultz was spot-on when he made all the adults in his *Peanuts* cartoons talk in unintelligible *waa-waa-waa* voices, because that's exactly what the average parent/child interaction looks like from the kid perspective.

From their angle, we use too many words to say what we need to say, everything we say sounds like we're mad, and we're usually interrupting some super important free play.

I know, from experience and conversations with all the parents around me, that every one of us feels ignored somewhere down the line. So while you may only be on the cusp of being tuned out by your kids because they're still super dependent on you for just about everything, the time will inevitably come when your voice starts sounding like the shrill of a fax machine signal when you accidentally dial into someone's fax line. But, like everything we go through with our kids, as they age and mature, the communication gap between us begins to close. Eventually, they come around and realize that it benefits them to listen to us. A lot. But it takes a while for them to accept that. For now, they just hear a lot of white noise from us.

At this point, though, when our kids are young, they're probably the most apt they're ever going to be to listen to us. Or at least that's what I've found with my own kids. They're still relatively young and innocent and dependent, and they still think we're the ones who know everything. Which is great in terms of us maintaining control. The older our kids get, though, the more their opinions take shape and their egos develop and they're less inclined to want or need our opinion. So it kinda feels like they just stop listening to us altogether. And that's not a good feeling if you're the one on the other end of the conversation.

We have to remember how we're sounding to our kids when we're trying to get their attention to do something we need them to do. Are we nagging them? Do we sound angry or annoyed? Are we threatening them for not paying attention to us? How we get *and keep* their attention is completely up to us. Honestly, after almost twenty years as a parent, I can say, without any hesitation, that I spent the majority of my time as a mom barking at my kids.

Ever take a step back and really listen to how you're talking to your kids? I'm guessing no. I know I didn't very often. But the truth is, if we all did a little self-reflecting once in a while, I think we'd see pretty clearly that we, as moms and dads, don't always come across the way we think we do. In our heads, we're gently coaxing our kids, but to them, we're full-on nagging, yelling, annoying, and pestering. And that's the crux of the communication problem between us and our kids. None of us really realizes how we sound to each other.

But there are things we can do to help ease the struggle on both sides.

We need to keep in mind that the kid brain gets easily engrossed. In everything. So even though we may want them to respond to us right away, they're not always able to, because that piece of their brain hasn't developed yet. Also, there's a great big difference between *want* and *need*. Which is why sometimes it's important for us to recognize whether what we're asking of them is what we really *need* or just something we really *want*. Because in case you haven't noticed, little kids aren't always the best transitioners.

Another thing to keep in mind is that a lot of the pushback we get from our kids at this age is driven by their need for attention. Which means that some of the time, they're not responding to us because they're trying to get our attention. And because they're so young and immature, they often can't differentiate between negative attention and positive attention. To them, attention is attention. To us, them not responding is just annoying.

One thing we can do pretty easily is remember that our kids *think* they know everything. They're sure they understand how to handle every situation and crisis and problem, even this young, and don't need our input, so they gradually start tuning us out as they start interacting with the rest of the world.

Something else that's critical in terms of communicating with our kids is to stay calm. Like, Buddha calm. Because an anxious parent and a defiant kid do *not* mesh well, I can tell you from experience. The minute I'd get riled up at my girls and they saw it, they'd know I was vulnerable and they'd tune me out even more. So the secret is to stay calm, even when you're not getting a response. Cool-like-the-other-side-of-the-pillow calm. Because if we're in a zen state of mind when we're trying to get our kids to cooperate, they'll be more inclined to listen.

Another trick you can try is making a game out of listening, at least at this age. If we make following directions and responding fun for our kids, then our kids are usually way more apt to get with the program. Make listening fun by putting a positive incentive on the other end. Maybe they get to stay up five minutes later or watch ten minutes more of their cartoon. Give them a carrot to reach for, and they'll be more eager to behave. You know, some good old-fashioned motivation. Which, by the way, is totally different than bribing our kids for listening and following directions. There's absolutely nothing wrong with incentivizing our kids for good behavior. In fact, it's incredibly effective. Because when we occasionally compensate them for doing what we need them to do, it helps them learn new skills.

This is not a bribe. I repeat: this is not a bribe.

Bribes, well, they're born out of manipulation and as a general rule are very, very bad. When we lob out a bribe as a way of modifying our kids' behavior, we've just given our kids complete control over the situation. As soon as they associate their negative behavior with getting a kickback, we've just lost the war. And that's simply because bribes are almost always given out under duress, when our last nerve is fraying and about to snap. It's a horrible option that we never want to use. Honestly, it shouldn't even be in our arsenal to begin with, because once we cross over into bribing our kids to listen or behave or communicate with us, we've just taken the first tragic step toward raising an entitled kid.

Remember, developing good communication with our kids is a process—a long, tedious, and totally imperfect process. We just have to be patient and stay the course. We have to work with our kids day in and day out to establish good communication patterns. And even though it's not easy, it can be done. And done well.

And if patience and tolerance and good role-modeling don't work, there's another trick we can whip out. We can give them a little taste of their own Robitussin and ignore them right back. We can refuse to answer them when they call us and let them feel, firsthand, what it's like to be ignored. We can start chopping veggies while they're trying to tell us something super important just so they can know the feeling of being dismissed. You get what I'm saying. *Teachable moments*, I believe they're called. Moments that we have to jump on whenever they present themselves because there is no better way of learning not to touch the hot stove than by getting a little burned.

And, OK, while this might be a slightly more juvenile and tit-for-tat method of fostering good communication with our kids, it's a killer strategy that works almost every time.

Like when both of my girls started repeatedly locking their bedroom doors for privacy. Instead of locking them only when they were getting changed, they started locking the door just to lock it every other time of the day. And whenever we'd knock to come in, they'd take their sweet little time getting up off their bed, walking over to the door, and unlocking it. To the point where it felt like we were standing outside their door waiting for ten minutes. So what did we start to do? We started locking our door. Constantly. Like in the morning and the afternoon and after dinner. And whenever they'd try to barge in (which they always did, because the knocking-out-of-consideration thing apparently didn't apply to them), our door was locked. Drove them crazy. They hated it. And every single time it happened, we'd just calmly say, "Getting dressed." Then we'd take our sweet time walking over to the door. And it didn't take too much of that to make an impression and get our point across, because, little by little, their doors were open and unlocked most of the day. (Plus I think they knew that if they didn't get with the program, their doorknobs were going to be taken off to help prove the same point.)

Either way, as long as we're patient and disciplined with how we handle communicating with our kids, we all eventually learn how to talk to each other. And to listen. (Which, I've learned, is equally as important.)

I mean, I'm not gonna lie to you; there's a huge learning curve associated with learning to talk to our kids. And we all definitely bash our heads against the wall a lot during this laying of the communication lines. Because everyone's learning how to talk to each other and how to listen, and that's just not easy. It's tricky from grown-up to grown-up and especially complicated from kid to adult.

There are huge gaps in the way we all understand each other. Unfortunately, us adults bear the brunt of that challenge. Because we're the ones trying to figure out ways to effectively talk to our kids and how to make them listen. And if you're like me, then sometimes you talk too much and your message is lost altogether. So from my perspective, it seems like once we realize that less is really more in terms of communication, then we start to see some real progress.

See, most **kids respond to the news and not the weather**. My kids certainly did at that age and still do today. And by that I mean be brief; be to the point; use simple, direct words; be very, very specific. Because most of them can't handle being saturated by directions or reprimands or lectures. Just call them out on their behavior or give them the direction you need them to follow and then step back and give them the chance to respond. I repeat: step back and give them at least a second to transition. Do *not* throw a hissy if they don't instantly bolt up from the play table all attentive and ready to serve. Because it won't happen.

And that's the thing: we have to remember that there's only so much processing our kids can do effectively—that any one of us can do effectively. Which is why the best piece of advice I can give anyone who's learning how to talk to their kids is to **just shut up and listen sometimes**. Not all the time, but sometimes for sure. Because the sooner we learn when to zip it and when to engage, the more effectively we'll be able to connect with our kids.

Oh yeah, and if absolutely none of that works (which is entirely possible), **just walk away**. Don't stand there hammering at your kid for the sake of resolving whatever conflict you're dealing with. (My own personal challenge.) That's because sometimes things need to stay unresolved for a little while until everyone can take a step back and reflect and, most importantly, cool down.

Me, I've never been good with leaving things open ended—certainly not with my kids. When we have arguments or disagreements, I'm always inclined to hash things out until we reach a resolution. So I keep saying the same thing, over and over and over. In ten different ways and for way too long, hoping that we'll settle things. But the problem with that is, my kids would almost always tune me out after a very short time (which is the tendency of most kids). And all of that talking becomes white noise that they can't process. And nothing gets accomplished.

That's why, oftentimes, sending everyone to their corners to regroup is the most effective solution. And although it sounds almost contradictory to walk away when we're trying to create a healthy dialogue with our kid, it's often the best approach. Why? Simple. It saves us from saying something we'll regret or from losing control or from getting mad. In other words, it saves us from ourselves. Because remember, we can't regret something we don't say or do. So stay cool and remember who your audience is—they're little kids. And if things get really dicey, excuse yourself and go lock yourself in the bathroom.

Myth #10

Myth: Our kids need to join as many extracurricular groups and clubs as possible to stay competitive.

Reality: Kids need free time to decompress, take a breath, and just be kids.

B ack in the day, when we were kids, we went to school, maybe we played an instrument, and if you were like me, you were one of only two girls in your town who played youth baseball. Besides that, we played outside until someone's mom blew a slide whistle at sundown that signaled us all to go home. Then we played Barbie or Matchbox cars or read actual books or maybe did Mad Libs. After that, we called it a day. And that was the way of the world. Now, though, our kids are racing from group to club to team to rehearsal, eating dinner on their lap in the car, and every parent is secretly praying for a monsoon to come so practice will be canceled.

Now that your kids are in school, you have to get used to the idea of them doing an awful lot more than just going back and forth to their classroom every day. Because up to now, most kids were in preschool a few hours a day and maybe at a Mom & Me swim class and that's it. Now, though, they're coming home from school and pulling on shin guards and karate uniforms and reaching for ballet slippers—all in the same day. And while it's great to see our kids busy and engaged and spending their time productively, they still need time to just be kids. Because without that, they're missing some really fundamental aspects of being young. Stuff that we don't always realize they're missing until we're forced to focus on it or it's too late.

Without the ability to relax and decompress in an unstructured way, our kids have no outlets for relieving stress or anxiety or solving problems and they become conditioned to look to us to fill all their time. And when we can't, or we're not available, they're lost.

So since I'm such a visual person, let's take a quick peek at the list I just pulled together of what I think our kids are missing when they're being shuttled from activity to activity without any downtime.

Without any free time, our kids:

- Can't learn how to entertain themselves and end up bugging the crap out of us.
- Can't learn to appreciate quieter, more solitary activities, like curling up with a good book (once they can read, of course), or drawing, or just being creative with everything that's around them.

- Can't have the chance to just daydream.
- Can't have the opportunity to decompress and process everything that they're exposed to every day.
- Can't get the chance to be inspired.
- Can't learn how to be independent.

Notice how I'm using the word *can't* a lot? Well, I'm doing that very deliberately because I'm trying to reinforce the idea that by *not* giving our kids the freedom to explore and be creative and rely on themselves to occupy at least a little of their time, we're setting them up to be codependent little robots who just cycle from activity to activity and can't think or entertain themselves on their own.

Our kids still need downtime and free playtime and freedom to make their own choices, in spite of the fact that most parents today feel ridiculous guilt over seeing their kids without anything to do. Even for a minute. I know I have. Probably because I, myself, prefer to be busy and productive, as a rule. Then again, I'm a grown-up. And I also appreciate my quiet time to do nothing. But kids aren't that evolved yet. And they do need their time to be structured. Just not all of it. Which is exactly why we need to teach our kids that it's OK to do nothing once in a while—it's OK for them to shut off their brains for a little while. In fact, it's necessary.

"There is a myth that doing nothing is wasting time, when it's actually extremely productive and essential," says Kathy Hirsh-Pasek, PhD, coauthor of *Einstein Never Used Flashcards: How Our Children Really Learn—and Why They Need to Play More and Memorize Less*. "During empty hours, kids explore the world at their own pace, develop their own unique set of interests, and indulge in the sort of fantasy play that will help them figure out how to create their own happiness, handle problems with others on their own, and sensibly manage their own time. That's a critical life skill."[6,7]

Because in case you haven't heard of it yet, there's this very real and damaging thing called *oversaturation*. In simple terms, it's when we, the parents, sign our kids up for every possible activity and fill every free second of our kid's day to ensure that they have no idle time. As a result, our kids are waaaay over-stimulated and they burn out. Fast. And ugly.

In my own experience, saturating our kids with too many activities is bad for the simple reason that, without any down-time to unwind, our kids have no time to decompress and process. It's like bleeding an old-fashioned radiator from the buildup of hot air so it doesn't explode. Well, our kids are like mini radiators who need to be allowed to vent to maintain balance in their little systems.

I've had countless conversations with other parents about how lost their kids are when they have even a little bit of free time. And I've had similar conversations with the kids themselves. I used to see kids dragging into school every morning, exhausted and frazzled from being in the car all weekend, traveling from field to field or court to court or practice to practice, and they hated it. Even though they loved the activity they were doing, they resented the fact that they were doing it all the time, which left them with little or no time to do anything else. And that constant, unrelenting pace inevitably led to a big crash and an even bigger burn.

I vividly remember one conversation I had with a kindergarten parent in my class after her daughter's full-on meltdown one Monday morning. Her daughter hadn't even made it out of the car at drop-off and she was already throwing a complete nutty. She refused to unbuckle her seatbelt and was swatting at her mom every time her mother reached for the buckle. And once her mom finally got the girl out of the car, the walk across the parking lot was equally as rough. The girl refused to walk. Just sat right down on the edge of the grass, crossed her arms and legs, and became dead weight. It was like she was at a sit-in for a No Nukes rally back in the '70s.

Eventually, it took a guidance counselor and her classroom teacher to convince her to come in the building. According to mom, she had spent the weekend at a travel soccer tournament with three dance recitals squished in between (one full dress rehearsal and two performances). Oh yeah, and she also had two lacrosse games because she was on that team too. The kid was fried.

Sound at all familiar?

So the question becomes: are we raising a generation of overachievers and Rhodes Scholars and future pro athletes or a bunch of frazzled overcommitted overachievers? I think we both know the answer.

The mentality today, at least among the parents I've seen in the school system and the parents I know personally, is to fill every free second of our kids' days with enough stimulation to ensure that they're equal to or ahead of their peers both academically and extracurricularly. I see it every day. First- or second- or third-grade kids coming out of their parent's car in the drop-off line lugging backpacks filled with tennis racquets, cleats tied onto the outside, carrying a lacrosse stick in one hand and a trumpet case in the other. Poor kids could barely get through the front door of the school.

I can't tell you how many of my friends' kids, or the kids I taught in the classroom, were so overcommitted that they barely knew their own names at the end of every day. They were completely strung out between travel soccer teams and swim teams and piano lessons and cooking classes that they were all frantically rushing back and forth from practice to rehearsal to practice. And you know what that kind of pace does? It creates tense, anxious parents. So while being involved in all of these groups and teams and clubs definitely kept the kids engaged, it also wore them down to little nubs.

I mean, don't get me wrong, I'm all for exposing kids to everything that's around them in terms of athletics and fine arts and languages and music and groups and clubs. Kids need to try on as many hats as they can while they're young to figure out what they like and what they don't like. (OK, maybe not hats, because of the lice thing. Ew.) But there comes a point when we have to pick and choose. We have to do it as the parents, and we have to teach our kids how to do it for themselves. Because even though we may be inclined and able to sign our kids up for every club or team we can find, we shouldn't.

It's actually OK to say no. In fact, it's necessary. It's on us to be the voice of reason when it comes to how our kids are spending their time. In the same way that we shouldn't be forcing them to be a lacrosse player or a flautist, we also shouldn't let them join three different sports teams when they're seven. We need to be actively setting limits for our kids. And not just with things like bedtimes and the amount of time they spend in front of the TV and the food they're eating but also with the kinds of commitments they make at a young age.

I know it's easy to get hung up on not wanting to disappoint our kids. Every parent wants to be popular with their children. But learning to say no is way more important than being popular. We have to be the ones who keep our kids and their schedules in check. And it's tough, because our kids are seeing their friends playing on multiple teams and being involved with Girl Scouts and drama clubs and hip-hop classes, and they want in. Why? Because they don't want to miss out. For the exact same reason that adults overextend ourselves. Because we don't want to be left out. We're seeing all the other moms and dads standing in line with their registration forms and feeling like we're doing our kids a disservice by not signing them up too. In truth, we're idiots. Because our kids need a break from responsibility just as much as we do.

And, ironically, according to the American Academy of Pediatrics, kids shouldn't specialize in any specific sport before they hit adolescence. They've got too many growing and developing tendons and ligaments that can be compromised by excessive overuse.[8] So I guess that means that kids should be playing sports at the elementary level for, uh, fun. Because when young kids cross over from playing recreational sports that are designed to move their bodies and give them a sense of being part of a team and a feel for sportsmanship into the realm of super-competitive sports, that's where the problems start. It's when too much pressure to perform is put on young kids that they cave.

And since we're on the subject of kids and sports and pressure, I need to talk for a second about participation trophies. And how much I dislike them and the counterproductive message they send. Because they are, in my opinion, ridiculous. These are the ribbons or medals or—heaven forbid—actual metal trophies that some youth sports teams give out to all their players *just* for showing up, putting on a uniform, and playing. Which is the very *last* reason we should be encouraging our kids to suit up and play every week.

To me, giving a kid a trophy is no different than giving my girls their diplomas just because they sat through every day of high school. It's bogus.

And I know from sharing the sidelines with many of them, that there's a population of moms and dads out there who are just as jazzed up about participation trophies as their kids are, for the simple fact that it's tangible proof that their kid plays a lot of sports. Not that they were a strong player or a good sport or a great teammate, but just because their kid laced up every week. That's it. And it's those same parents who mandate that their kids play a sport every season, sometimes two, just to stay competitive. They could care less if their kid liked basketball or not or was good at it or not, they just wanted them on the team for the sake of being involved.

Because just in case you haven't learned this yourself yet, we're not all winners. And we're not supposed to be. There's always going to be someone out there who jumps higher or runs faster or throws further than us or our kid. And to pretend otherwise is setting our kids up for a huge boot to the face as they grow up and expect to get recognized for every little teeny tiny thing they ever do. Cause it's not reality.

I've been a cross country coach to over one hundred fourth-, fifth-, and sixth-grade girls every spring and fall for the last five years and I can tell you that none of them cares about medals or prizes or podiums. That's because the women I coach with have taught our girls that winning or losing doesn't matter. What matters is that you're in the game. And I'm happy to report that every single girl is out there giving her best effort, not caring about her pace or the hardware she may or may not get at the finish. They're out there feeling proud to be giving their best effort. And that's it.

Now should our kids get recognized for being a member of a team and being a contributor to that team whether they score the winning point or not? Whether they're team captain or not? Of course they should. But that kind of acknowledgment should come in the form of a high-five from their coach or a team shirt or maybe a Blow-Pop. Not a trophy or a ribbon or a plaque. If you want to raise a little narcissist who thinks that everything she does is amazing, be my guest. But the reality is, we need to impart to our kids that sometimes we win and sometimes we lose, but either way, it's just about being able to play the game.

For instance . . . My now-nineteen-year-old daughter played soccer from the time she was five until she went to high school. That's a lotta soccer. She played every position from goalie to midfielder to striker. (She got around a lot, but in a good way). She hardly missed a practice, loved her teammates, and worked her butt off during every game. And in almost nine years on the field, the kid never scored a single goal. Not one in all those years in a regular-season game. And she couldn't have cared less. Which, at the end of the day, is what we should all really want. She just loved being a part of a team—part of something bigger than just herself. She loved the camaraderie and the feeling of learning each other's rhythms and strengths and weaknesses. And it ultimately laid the foundation for her wanting to be part of a team in high school. Because she realized that even though she never scored even one point for her team, she had plenty of assists that turned into goals that turned into wins. And that showed her that every player has value when you're all working together towards the same endgame.

So do we want our kids to learn the feeling of being part of a team or a group or a club? Absolutely. Being part of something larger than just ourselves is an essential part of growing up. It speaks to teamwork and collaboration and flexibility. It teaches us how to communicate and builds self-esteem. It helps us learn how to build relationships. All invaluable lessons. But knowing when enough is enough is on us. Saying no to the third travel field hockey team is on us. Teaching our kids that quality is greater than quantity is on us. And the meltdown that will come from us overscheduling them is squarely on us.

Myth #11

Myth: Kids should be seen and not heard.

Reality: A healthy sense of sarcasm is a gift.

There's nothing worse, in my opinion, than a snarky, loudmouthed kid who makes inappropriate comments and makes you want to pretend that you're not actually her parents. But show me a kid who can really banter with the big boys and understands the fine art of sarcasm, and *that's* the one I want to hang with. *That's* the one I'm proud to call my own.

Teaching our kids the difference between being playfully and appropriately sarcastic and being fresh and completely rude, though, is tough. But it *can* be done. And when it's done successfully, it's one of the most charming qualities you'll love about your kids. Because contrary to the old-school philosophy of kids needing to be seen and not heard, allowing and encouraging a child to be witty and playful can enable that child to grow into an adult who can carry themselves in social situations and engage the people around them. And do it well. So it's a life skill, as far as I'm concerned—**a really valuable life skill.**

Stay with me here and don't panic—testing boundaries through communication and language is totally age appropriate right now. It's just another way our kids are coming into their own.

Let me explain why I feel so strongly about the benefits of raising a child with a healthy sense of sarcasm. But before I do, it's important to clearly define the true essence of sarcasm. First of all, according to my bud Oscar Wilde, "sarcasm is the lowest form of wit but the highest form of intelligence." So right there, you know it's got some teeth.

In simplest terms, and according to *Merriam-Webster*, sarcasm is "the use of words that mean the opposite of what you really want to say . . . especially in order to be . . . funny." Now, the extended definition includes words like *ironic* and *insult* and *irritation*, but that's not the kind of sarcasm I'm talking about here. What I'm talking about is the kind that's meant to be a harmless, nonoffensive joke. Because the last thing I'd suggest is that we teach our kids how to mock other people or convey contempt. That would be bad.

What I *am* suggesting is that there are some real hidden benefits to raising a kid who is quick witted. For example, when tossed out with thoughtfulness and self-control, sarcasm can enhance your child's creativity because they're forced to think more abstractly. In other words, it stimulates the creative thinking process. Not to mention that they have to be able to process their exchanges with people much faster than in just regular conversation.

Remember, at our core, human beings are social animals. Most of us thrive on contact and communication with other people. And because of that, our society has evolved into a culture of quick thinkers. Believe it or not, *Smithsonian Magazine* actually says, "Children understand and use sarcasm by the time they get to kindergarten."[9] Which means that it's our responsibility as parents to raise kids who can keep up, intellectually, with the people around them. We need to kindle their sense of humor early on so they can understand and benefit from how humor and sarcasm play into the world they're growing into.

In today's culture, raising a kid who can survive and thrive in a world where sarcasm has become mainstream is essential. And I can actually back that up, thanks to John Haiman, a linguist at Macalaster College in Minnesota, who agrees that "sarcasm is practically the primary language in today's society."[10] Yeppers, it's true. So in an effort to prepare our kids to be able to successfully engage in today's competitive world, they need to be fluent banterers. It's a fact.

According to KidsHealth.org, "a good sense of humor is a tool that our kids will rely on throughout life." They say that "kids with a well-developed sense of humor are happier and more optimistic, have higher self-esteem, and can handle differences (their own and others')well."[11] And in my experience both as a mom and as an educator, they're right.

Some of the most well-adjusted kids (and adults) I know have an incredible sense of humor. And as far as I'm concerned, it just adds to their charm because they know how to make people laugh and think and feel at ease.

Some of my favorite kids over the years have been the ones who knew how to be funny and could comfortably engage with the other kids around them. They weren't threatening or aloof or mocking; they were easygoing, and their sense of humor put everyone around them at ease.

That's because humor does a lot of things, actually. It teaches our kids to be playful and lighthearted. It encourages them to be quick on their feet. It enables them to think multidimensionally and be critical thinkers. And it can ward off things like moodiness and depression. Not to mention that laughter, in general, is super beneficial because it actually oxygenates the blood and improves brain function. Oh, and it helps defuse things like kid meltdowns. (Really hard for your second grader to throw the remote at you if she's peeing herself laughing.)

In the same way that learning to play music or speak a foreign language or painting expands our children's learning capabilities, so too does sarcasm. (Crazy, right?!) But it's like calisthenics for their brains. I mean, we encourage our kids to play sports as a form of exercise and learn an instrument to stimulate their neural processing, so doesn't it make perfect sense that we exercise their sense of humor, too? Well, duh.

See, when Dave and I were first married, we were friends with this couple who had a six-year-old son. Super cute kid. He had a sense of humor like an edgy stand-up comic, and we loved that about him. Because he was funny but appropriate and everyone loved being around him.

Even at six, he got the essence of sarcasm. He was quick witted and sharp as hell, and we used to cross our fingers that when we had kids of our own, they'd have a sense of humor just like him. Because as far as we were concerned, having a kid with a good sense of humor was a gift. We agreed then that we were going to do our best work someday raising our kids to be able to hold their own in a sarcastic interchange. And almost twenty years and two kids later, I'm proud and happy to report that we've raised exceptionally funny daughters (biased mother's opinion, of course). Both of our girls can hold their own in any sarcastic conversation. They know how to sling it, how to receive it, and how to temper it, both with their friends and with ours. And judging by how many comments we've gotten over the years about how funny our kids can be, I'm confident we've done right by them by helping them to enhance this part of their personality.

I know that historically, most new parents pray that their kids are well behaved and stay under the radar in social situations. So I realize that good sarcasm probably isn't on most parents' top ten list of desired kid traits, but I think it should be. It really *is* ok to embrace having a kid with a sharp sense of humor. It's good for them and good for you because it's something you can bond over, believe it or not. We do with our girls. In fact, it's almost like a contest in our family to see who can be the most sarcastic. (Obviously, slightly different rules of sarcastic engagement apply to your immediate family and friends than the rest of the general population.) Your family and friends will *get* you. And while the rest of the world may or may not, peoples' reaction to our sarcasm is a definite litmus test that helps us gauge which people are most like us and who we belong with for the long haul.

I vividly recall the first real conversation we had about the type of kids we hoped to have and how both of us wished that they'd be born with whatever magical DNA generates a healthy sense of sarcasm. You know, that certain gene that a person's born with that gives them perfect comedic timing. Well, we wanted that kid. And we felt pretty confident, at least from a DNA standpoint, that between the two of us, we had a dominant-enough DNA sequence to ensure that our kids would be at least mildly sarcastic.

We always hoped that our kids would develop a healthy, appropriate sense of comedic timing. Because as far as I'm concerned, there's absolutely nothing more gratifying than watching one of my daughters toss out an expertly crafted joke or one-liner that has the ability to make people laugh (and think). It's a real gift, and any parent should be proud to have a child with that kind of social skill. I know I am.

We've actually felt legitimate pride in our kids' ability to recognize and deliver a solidly ironic comment. Because not everyone can. Not everyone is wired to give or receive sarcastic humor. Just like not everyone is born with rhythm or the ability to hit a high note or pick up a guitar and just play. There's certain stuff we're born with, and an edgy sense of humor is one of them.

When our kids are young, they've got no filter. That's a given. They hear stuff, they imitate it, and they get laughs and attention wherever and however they can. And that's not always a good thing. But sarcasm can be cultivated, under the right conditions, and enhanced with guidance and support from loving sarcastic parents.

Well, part of it is genetic, sure. Some people are just inherently more sarcastic and quick on their feet, while others take some real grooming. And like most things, it can be learned with time and effort.

I do realize that it sounds a little ridiculous to actually *hope* your kids are sarcastic, but you have to understand that Dave and I both come from incredibly saucy families who love to hurl it every which way, so it just seemed natural for us to cross our fingers and hope that any kids we had would be little wisenheimers. Because amongst our families, the more you sling it, the more you love the slingee. And that's just as true with our friends.

Not to mention the fact that there have been actual studies done that support the idea that sarcastic people are more creative than nonsarcastic types. Yep. It's true. In Eric Fluckey's *Huffington Post* article "Why Sarcasm Is So Great," he wrote that scientists from Harvard, Columbia, and INSEAD Business School just *had* to learn if sarcasm had any effects on a person's cognitive abilities. So much so that they ran an actual experiment. (Love that that's what they spent their time and resources evaluating.) And the people in the test groups who had given or received sarcastic remarks in conversations outperformed those who didn't. In fact, they were found to be about three times more creative. Because, Fluckey says, both the giver and the receiver had to mentally work out the contradictory nature of sarcasm for it to be effective. The mental processes involved in the interpretation and delivery seemed to flame the creative spark.[12]

Now, don't get me wrong; I'm well aware that there is, and should be, a very distinct line between healthy, appropriately timed, harmless sarcasm and full-on snarkiness. That's why Dave and I raised our kids to know the difference. Because we both recognize that it's all too easy for people, especially kids, to cross the line and turn an innocent remark that's designed to be funny into something rude and chafing. Which is definitely not OK.

The problem is, sarcasm has a bad rap. People hear the word and it has a negative connotation because the primary definition of the word is *the use of irony to mock or convey contempt.* And there's nothing at all charming about being disrespectful. That said, though, there's more than one meaning of the word. Actually, according to YourDictionary.com, sarcasm also means *the use of irony to make a joke.* And there's nothing socially wrong with making a joke, right?

I will admit, though, now that my girls are in high school and college, that it would be refreshing, every once in a while, if they slid a normal comment into at least one conversation every day. Because the irony is that we may have created our own little monsters in some small way by harnessing and developing the sarcasm gene. But all things being equal, I wouldn't have it any other way.

We need to embrace and nurture all the beautiful qualities in our children, and this trait is no different.

So the trick is to coach our kids on where and when sarcasm is applicable in their everyday lives. Start small, in the confines of the house. Take a few shots to the chin before you expose them to other people. Let them settle into a groove first and get a feel for what they can and can't say. Then, gradually, once they get their sea legs, let them loose on the rest of the world.

And if anyone judges you for having appropriately sarcastic kids, just tell them you're encouraging your kids to exercise their sarcastic side and they should be doing the same. (Just remember to say it in an ironic-sounding tone.)

Myth #12

Myth: Technology is wrecking our kids.

Reality: Our technology-driven world necessitates technology-savvy kids.

Back in the day, when we were all kids, how we entertained ourselves was decidedly different than how our kids entertain themselves today. When we were young, we had stuff like markers and colored paper and skateboards and VHS tapes. We played HORSE. We played Barbie (making Ken and Barbie kiss, of course). We actually played catch and climbed trees (in some cases, falling out of them). With the exception of maybe an Atari 2600 that some kid got for his bar mitzvah, that was pretty much the extent of our recreation outlets. And most everything we did had nothing whatsoever to do with technology or screens. Life was simpler in a lot of ways. But, as civilizations do, we evolved. And our kids evolved right along with us.

Today's kids live in an entirely different world than we did. They're inundated with iPads and iPhones and Xboxes and tablets and handheld gaming systems and touchscreens. They're clicking and dragging and swiping their little brains out. And they have an endless array of super-slick equipment to choose from to occupy their time. The most obvious downside of which is that all those options are keeping them from all the old-fashioned ways of spending their free time. (Not to mention cutting into all the time they could be spending with us.)

And even though all this technology represents a different kind of fun factor to our kids, unrivaled by anything we had growing up, the reality is that it's taking them away from the pickup games and the bike rides and the afternoons running around playing Man Hunt in the neighborhood. Now, with technology being so accessible, our kids have the ability, even at a really young age, to engross themselves in games and media that can stream forever. Like, for-ever. And that's something we can't relate to because we didn't grow up in a digital world. The most we could do was sit in front of the TV all day and night until the station stopped broadcasting at midnight. (Big night!) Otherwise, we could get lost in books (*if* we were readers, unlike myself). Beyond that, we had to find things to do. We had to get creative.

But our kids don't have to get creative in the same ways we did. All the activities they want are in an app or on a website, just a quick click away. All the thinking is gone. And since the content is never ending, it's like they've got a built-in buddy and babysitter 24/7. They've got constant companionship and entertainment without ever having to leave their room.

The fact is, we're vying pretty heavily for our kids' attention in ways that our parents never had to because the gravitational pull of all this technology is more or less irresistible to today's kids. And because they're being exposed to all these electronics earlier and earlier, they're getting immersed in technology almost as soon as they can walk and talk. And that presents a big problem for us. Because it's all they know.

They can go anywhere, entertain themselves twenty-four hours a day, and, theoretically, never leave the couch while they're doing it. All with pocket-size devices that fit perfectly in their hot little hands. But the downside to that is that they're not using their bodies to physically go *anywhere*. With all the glitzy, engaging gadgets all around them, our kids are being lured away from all of the traditional kinds of entertainment, like getting out and exercising and using their own imagination. They're spending less and less time talking to each other face-to-face or over the phone and more and more time secluded and staring down at some kind of screen. They're joining online gaming communities and playing virtually instead of getting outside and running around and getting sweaty and using their bodies. And that's not good.

So, the big question on every parent's mind is: *Is technology wrecking our kids?* Is all this screen time damaging them intellectually and emotionally and physically and stunting their growth and frying their brains? Not easy questions to answer, because the answer really depends almost exclusively on how we handle the amount of time they spend on all their devices.

If we let our kids lock themselves in their bedroom and be digital all day, like a lot of young kids would love to do, then, in addition to being severely Vitamin D deficient, our kids would have zero muscle tone, no interpersonal communication skills, and no endurance whatsoever. They'd basically be lonely, isolated little hermits with really, really pale skin.

When my kids were young and they had their first cell phones, I felt an immeasurable sense of relief that I could reach out and connect with them any time I needed them. And vice versa. As a mom, it was like having the world's longest umbilical cord attached to both of my kids. I always had the ability to reach out to them, unless, of course, one of them was being snarky and turned off their location services. (Oh yeah, that happened.) There's an incredible comfort level that comes with being able to stay connected. That's the true upside with all this technology.

Keep in mind that my girls grew up just on the cusp of the social media explosion—stuff like Facebook and Twitter were barely emerging when they were young. (Thank God.) All they had were basic multiplayer online games like Club Penguin and Webkinz, little virtual worlds where they could goof around with other kids in a cutesy little cyberworld filled with limited chat capabilities and comic strip characters. (Not a lot to worry about in Webkinz World.) But even in spite of the fact that most age-appropriate games available at that time were pretty rudimentary, my oldest daughter still managed to lose a few shades of skin pigment hanging out in her room playing those games. And it wasn't until we saw how affected she was by direct sunlight when we opened her curtains in the middle of the day that we realized she was a little too consumed. Suffice it to say we pulled the plug, threw her outside in the backyard, and made her climb some trees and breathe in some fresh air. And within a short time, she was able to see how much she was missing by being indoors on her computer for hours at a time.

But that's the fundamental problem with technology: knowing when enough is enough. And since each kid is so different, those limits vary from household to household. Because some kids have the natural ability to self-regulate better than others. Some kids are just more attracted to technology than others. And those are the ones who need a little extra kick in the butt to unplug.

And as far as cell phones were concerned, they both got basic flip phones when they hit the fourth grade, around age nine. They didn't have texting or Internet capabilities. All they had was the ability to send and receive calls. That's it. And that was true of most of their little friends.

Now, though, even just a handful of years later, so much has changed. Today, kids are using cell phones at an even earlier age. Gone are the days of little kids getting base-model cell phones just to be able to check in with mommy and daddy after school. That's been replaced by grammar school kids walking around with the newest generation iPhone that's been pimped out with unlimited data and texting. I'd see eight-, nine-, and ten-year-old kids walking past me in the pickup line wearing a two-hundred-dollar pair of Beats headphones and carrying a newer, more powerful cell phone than I had in my purse.

But that's how much and how fast times are changing. According to a 2015 survey in *Child Guide Magazine*, a resource guide for parents, the average American child gets their first cell phone when they're six years old.[13] Six years old! And even though that sounds ridiculously young, it's becoming more and more mainstream to see little kids walking around with phablets bigger than their own heads. They all have them. And don't forget, if we're noticing what they have, you can bet that your kids are noticing who has what too. Therein lies the problem.

Remember, our kids are the first real generation to grow up in the Digital Age. And what that means is that they've grown up in a digital world, where everyone's connected and there's a cell phone in every back pocket. That's just the world we're living in. The world *they're* living in.

So it's up to us to help them learn to balance time on electronics with time on everything else. Because as our kids get older, they're faced with a very different kind of addiction than we had growing up. They're battling the constant temptation of devices and screens and social media in ways that most of us can't even understand. Because it didn't exist when we were kids.

The choices we had for things to occupy our time twenty or thirty years ago could be equated to shopping at the Gap versus shopping at Macy's—we just didn't have as many options, unlike our kids. But we were always entertained, even in spite of the limited choices we had when we were the kids. Ignorance was bliss, I guess.

As the parents of the first kids to be raised in a totally technology-driven world, we're in uncharted territory. We're pioneers raising the first generation of tech-savvy kids. And most of us are making up the rules as we go along. Not to mention trying to keep up with the technology learning curve. Not only do we have to know what our kids are doing online and on their phones, but we've also got to be able to navigate it ourselves. And that can be pretty intimidating for new parents. Which is exactly why we can't stress out too much about our kids being connected and being online. It's part of their culture. Part of the world they're growing up in.

We have to remind ourselves every day that our kids never grew up talking on the phone to their friends like we did. Sad as it is for those of us who grew up talking to our friends on the phone, today's digital generation is interacting with each other in very different ways. Perfect example: my girls literally laugh at me when I suggest that they pick up the phone and call their friends. *No one calls anyone, Mom*, they both say. And it's true: they don't. Instead, they Snapchat and post and tweet and tag. It's different. Very, very different. They've got computers in every classroom; they're doing schoolwork on their phones; they're using devices in school every day. This is the new world.

Now, look, I'm a supporter of all the technology around us. Because it's definitely got its obvious benefits. Above all, it allows us all to stay connected—a super critical factor for parents wanting to keep tabs on our kids. Technology also gives our kids unlimited platforms to explore their creativity. Whether they're into art or music or design or photography or anything else they can think of, they have an entire world of resources sitting only a click away. But I'm also a big believer in limits. Because limits are the key to ensuring that our kids keep their priorities straight from an early age. Everything in moderation, right?

In our house, we had a no-devices-at-the-dinner-table rule that we still have today. And it was modeled straight from the top. None of us were allowed to pull out a phone or a Nintendo DS at the kitchen table, in a restaurant, or at a friend's house, and that was just the rule. Period. Still is. And believe me, my kids notice who does and who doesn't whenever we go out. They also know never to *dare* having a conversation with me while looking at a screen. They wouldn't dream of it. And that's because it's just rude. We consider it a courtesy thing, something that's nonnegotiable.

Unfortunately, we can only fight the fight so far because the reality is that we live in a digital world where our kids are being expected to use technology at school and at work and as a means of staying connected. It's just how our society has evolved. But we still have the ability as parents to mandate certain rules, even in spite of what other people are doing around us. It's our job to set limits with our kids and ensure that they grow up knowing that technology has a very specific place and role in our world. In other words, we absolutely have to be willing to rip that phone or controller out of their hands if they're not toeing the line. That's how we make it work. That's how we make them understand.

So how young is too young for all of this technology? Well, that's a tough one because kids are seeming more mature and savvy at younger and younger ages nowadays.

Look, with my kids, social media wasn't quite mainstream yet when they were young. We had *that* going for us. But the world is changing so quickly. Just five years ago, kids started getting iPhones, even in the lower grades like third and fourth. But nine years ago, as recently as 2006, the iPhone didn't even exist. There was less for us to learn, so keeping up with them was doable. Now, though, learning all the new apps and interfaces is like learning Latin from scratch in a weekend. Take the app that's white hot right now as I'm sitting here writing, Pokémon GO. It's been released for less than a week, and it's already changed the world—partly for the better and partly for the worse. It's bringing kids together in an active way, but they're also obsessing over it.

Remember, the potential for addiction with these things is always there, just under the surface. Which is why we have to stay on top of what they're doing and how long they're doing it. We have to assert our authority and our ability to take all this stuff away in a blink. Because without any expectations or limit-setting, most kids just don't have the capacity to self-regulate.

Even in our family, where Dave worked for Microsoft for years and we were always surrounded by the newest, hottest technology, we knew how important limits were for our girls. We knew that a virtual world, no matter how enticing and exciting, could never be a replacement for the real world. Which is exactly why we insisted that our kids get on Razor scooters and bikes and swing sets and climb trees and hike and leave their devices behind.

So we make rules and enforce them. We teach our kids, at an early age, not to be dependent on devices. We teach them to look up, often, so they don't miss the world around them. We make sure they know how to pick up all the social and emotional cues around them even though they have technology in their hands. We remind them that texting us or their friends from the other room is *not* OK. (Unless, of course, you need them to turn down the TV and you're all comfy in the bedroom and they're in the living room. In that case, it's totally fine.)

I actually had a parent come to me, when my girls were in grammar school, complaining that she couldn't get her own girls to break away from their phones. She whined and moaned to me about how constantly distracted they were and had no idea whatsoever how to manage their overindulgence. To which I reminded her (sans the dope slap that I really wanted to give her) that *she* was the parent. *She* was the one who made the rules and bought the phones, and *she* paid for the cell service. And I think it was a defining moment for her because I openly called her out on dropping the ball as a parent. I reminded her that how her kids used or abused the technology *she* gave them was on her.

Let me say again: it's up to us and us alone to prevent technology from ruining our kids. And in spite of how challenging it might look to maintain a healthy balance with all this stuff in their lives, it's really not all that hard. We just have to **hold the line**, no matter what. We carve out family time and time for books and time for creativity and time for exercise, and technology becomes just another little thing that we fit into our day-to-day world. It fits in the way *we* tell them it fits in. We make the rules. And if they're not OK with that (because they *will* push back, them being kids and all), then we pull the plug and hand them a bunch of rocks to play with. And they'll get with the program eventually.

Myth #13

Myth: My kids are too immature/too little for chores.

Reality: There are no free rides.

I'm not sure who said it first or why (not that it matters), but whomever it was that came up with the line about there being no free rides is my hero. Because it's true in every aspect of our lives, especially where kids are concerned. We all need to learn how to pull our own weight, both in our personal and our professional worlds, as much for ourselves and our own sense of independence as for the people we interact with along the way. And the earlier we learn that, the better off we are in the long run. Which is exactly why one of the best things we can give to our kids is a sense of ownership and responsibility. In fact, the sooner we do that, the better.

Otherwise, we're raising a generation of freeloaders. And we can't be doing that, now, can we?

I know, I know; we don't want to impose on our cute little munchkins to do too much too soon. I mean, they're so little and so inexperienced and so fragile, right? Uh, wrong. Wrong, wrong, wrong. Our kids are *way* more capable than we realize way earlier than we think they are. We're just so used to caring for them and coddling them and wiping their chins (and butts) for those first handful of years that we often don't recognize when they're ready to start taking on some age-appropriate responsibilities. We see them as helpless little babies who need hand-holding, who have to keep their hands away from the stovetop, and who shouldn't help put the china away. And while that's true to a point, with the right guidance, our kids can also be real contributors if we give them a chance. Without things like chores and regular tasks, our kids become entitled. And an entitled kid is B-A-D. Because an entitled kid becomes an entitled adult. And that's even worse.

With my kids, we threw chores at them almost from the time they could walk and talk. We wanted them to feel like valuable little members of our family, so we involved them in as much of the day-to-day chores and routines as we could so they'd have a feeling of ownership in the home they were growing up in. You know, as a way of developing a sense of pride in themselves and where they came from.

We handed out the reasonable stuff in the beginning (when they were around four or five), like putting their dishes in the dishwasher and clothes in the hamper and trying to get themselves dressed (I stress *trying*, because watching a four-year-old try to navigate a pair of tights on her own is dicey). Then, when they got a little older (like six or seven), we turned up the heat and doled out the more advanced, highly complex stuff like feeding and walking the dog and bed-making and running loads of laundry. Expanding their repertoire, you know?

Now, relax; we weren't exploiting any child labor laws. We were just involving our girls in our day-to-day family routines so they'd get a sense, early on, of how to manage the life skills that everyone needs to master by the time they go out on their own. And we started when they were young because, let's face it, there's a lot to learn and the learning curve is wide. Kids don't come out of the womb knowing how to bake the perfect chocolate chip cookie with just the right amount of chew factor, or properly clean the dryer filter, or correctly fold a fitted sheet. Those things all have to be practiced over and over again. For years. Which is exactly why starting them early eases kids into the routine of doing these things regularly.

It's also to our advantage to let our kids get a feel for what we have to do every day as parents. Because I don't know about you, but for the longest time, my kids thought a pile of neatly folded laundry just spontaneously appeared on the corner of their bureau every week. Or that a team of sneaky little ninja elves snuck into their rooms every Sunday morning and changed their sheets, leaving them crisp and smelling lemony fresh. Or that food cooked itself and found its way to the kitchen table every day. Or that groceries instinctively knew how to travel from the supermarket into our fridge—all by themselves. We need to prove to our kids that all of this stuff happens manually, not magically. And the best way for them to understand that is by rolling their little sleeves up and getting their noses in there.

By the time I was ten years old, my dad had taught me how to use a lawnmower, how to pump gas at the gas station, how to change a flat, how to pump up my own bike tires . . . the list is long. And my mom did the same, teaching me how to Con-Tact paper my dollhouse walls (indispensable life skill), how to bake a level birthday cake, how to water the flowers without drowning them. That list was just as long. And learning all those things just made me want to learn more things. Because I found knowledge to be power.

I can remember being seven or eight, eating at my mom and dad's favorite restaurant, begging them and our regular wait-ress to give me a job. All I wanted was my own little spiral order notebook and white half-apron. I wanted to clear tables and take orders and wash dishes. Hell, I would've cleaned out toilet bowls just to say I had a job. And it wasn't even about earning money; I just wanted a purpose. (Again, don't ask me why. I was a bit stupid back in the day.)

So what did my parents do? After hearing me beg for a job week after week, they secretly arranged with the waitress and the owner to let me "work" in the kitchen. (Big air quotes around the word *work*.) And the night the waitress called me into the kitchen to "tell me something" was a defining moment for me. Because when I walked into the kitchen and she and the cooks handed me a little white apron and a notebook from the Five & Dime Store, I was finally being taken seriously. Which is really all most little kids want anyway.

They let me take peoples' orders (those people being my parents); they let me stack dishes and fold napkins and put ice in the glasses. In my head, though, it felt like they were trusting me with nuclear launch codes—that's how grown up I felt. And because of that, I wanted to do the best job humanly possible. Because, to me, their faith in my ability to do the job (any job) inspired me. And it gave me the confidence to believe I could do it, and that got me inspired. For a kid, that's big. And I've been inspired to work hard ever since.

Sure, kids balk, at times. God knows my kids do. But they're kids, and that's what kids do. Because they just don't understand that all these seemingly mundane little chores we ask them to do serve a purpose. They're building up to something. Doing something as simple as taking the dog out or putting away the laundry every day gives our kids the foundation for doing bigger, more impactful things for themselves and others down the line. And since it's our job to parent our kids, keeping them on task, even when they don't want to be, is just one of the many ways we do it.

Few things, in my opinion, are more important than learning how to fend for ourselves. Because if we don't learn how to do that, then how can we possibly ever learn how to take care of anyone else? And that's one of the main reasons why chores are so valuable. These seemingly tedious little tasks actually have a big purpose when we have our kids do them. By having them do tasks over and over and over, for years, we teach our kids to be self-sufficient by the time they go out in the world on their own.

It's only when our kids have learned a solid work ethic at home and they understand the benefits of pitching in and helping out and pulling their weight that we know we've done our job well. Helping out around the house is a simple and easy way for our kids to develop a sense of being a team player. And there's no team more important than the Home Team.

Until then, we need to hammer at them with this stuff so they understand that learning to keep their room clean is a life skill. Putting their dishes in the dishwasher is a life skill. Knowing how to make their whites *super* white is a life skill. And learning how to be an active contributor in life starts at home. But getting them to understand that and cooperate, though, can be a struggle. Because what kid would ever opt to do chores over playing Xbox or playing hoops or watching Netflix? No kid, that's who. Which is exactly why we exposed our kids early on to the world of chores. We wanted to weave it into their lives from the time they were little to avoid any real shock to their system when they got older.

By age five, our girls were doing hospital corners on their beds (not really, but that would've been impressive, right?), taking in groceries from the car, setting and clearing the dinner table, and helping cook meals. And the main reason why we wanted them to get comfortable doing all the little day-to-day things is because you never fully understand what it takes to do something unless you've done it yourself. You also have no way of empathizing with someone unless you've walked in their shoes. Like, oh, I don't know, a mom or a dad. And a great way to do that is to let our kids do a little bit of heavy lifting to give them a healthy dose of perspective.

This is also around the time when it's smart to consider using an allowance as an incentive for doing regular work around the house. Our kids were too young for any kind of real job like babysitting or a paper route, but they were definitely capable of consistently managing some chores around the house. So as a way of exposing them to what it means to work for your money, we started giving them around $5 a week for walking the dog and doing things like dishes and taking out trash. Just a little bit of pocket money that made them feel grown up and responsible. And it worked, because they learned early on what it felt like to earn their own money. Money that didn't always come right away, either, because we'd give them their allowance at the end of the week, after they did all their chores.

Granted, there were plenty of times when they blacked out and completely forgot that a bathrobe or towel went on the hook on the back of the bathroom door that was specifically designed to hold them. They were kids, after all. They needed to be pushed just like most kids do. But what I've found, now that my kids are older and self-sufficient and both holding down jobs, is that they love the feeling of being self-reliant. They actually love being productive and knowing how to take care of themselves. And yours will too, eventually.

The key is to start small with our kids. But we start. I say again, **we need to start**. We have to teach them that being a contributor at home isn't just great because it lightens mommy and daddy's load around the house but because they're going to feel really good about helping out. And that the value of their contribution isn't measured by the size and scope of the chore they do but, instead, by how much it helps everyone around them.

The problem often is, though, that devoting the time it takes to show them what to do in the first place isn't always easy. Because, as we all know way too well, young kids need to be supervised almost every waking second. And even though they don't think they do, they need a certain amount of hand-holding when they're learning new things.

Now, in theory, delegating responsibilities around the house makes our load lighter. In theory. But it doesn't always start out that way. Initially, when we're teaching our kids how to help us cook or do laundry or wash dishes, we need to be prepared to build in some training time. But that's the case with learning anything new. And that's definitely the case with kids.

But that extra investment of our time teaching our kids how to navigate the kitchen or the laundry room is *way* worth it on the back end; trust me. Think of it like potty training. I know, in some ways, it was almost easier to let our kids pee and poop in a diaper that kept everything self-contained than to lock ourselves in the house for a week and train our son how to use the potty like a big boy. I have countless friends who prolonged getting their daughter into big girl undies just because they didn't want to have to deal with the training process. So, I get it: it's sometimes easier to just keep it simple. But we're not doing anyone any favors, least of all our kids. Because the sooner we empower them to think and do for themselves, the more capable and confident they'll be in the end.

Truth is, some parents view giving their kids chores as an inconvenience because they have to teach and supervise them until the kids can manage tasks on their own. But those same parents aren't thinking long-term. They don't realize that, eventually, a little bit of effort on the front end almost always translates to a more self-sufficient kid on the back end.

The simple fact is that chores are good for our kids, even though our kids will insist that they aren't. Because being given adult responsibilities is empowering when we're young. It's a gesture of good faith on our part to show them that we trust them to handle real life stuff and acknowledge that they're mature—or at least matur*ing*. That's how I always felt, anyway. I loved the idea of working from as early as I can remember. I always wanted a job. Always wanted to be trusted to do grown-up things. (Don't ask me why. I was clearly just a confused kid who didn't recognize how good I had it as a child with little to no real responsibility. Youth . . . it's wasted on the young.)

And if we're going to be successful at teaching our kids how to start fending for themselves and giving back at home, then we have to resist the urge most of us have to do everything for them. It's actually critical. Because the longer we hand-hold, the tougher it is for our kids to let go and stand on their own. And that's the true endgame with parenting. I know at this point, when our kids are so young and still so dependent on us for so much, it's hard to ever imagine that the time will come when they'll be able to live life on their own. But it comes. And it comes fast.

So here's what *not* to do . . . don't tell your daughter you don't need her help chopping veggies just because you're afraid she might cut herself. All of their future salad preparation depends on it. Plus, she needs to know how to cut stuff if she's going to be able to use her own kitchen someday. And don't forget: chores are gender neutral. Our daughters are just as capable of shoveling snow and raking leaves as our sons are. And our sons are just as able to switch and fold the laundry and load the dishwasher as our daughters.

The other important trap not to fall into is being too much of a perfectionist to hand chores off to our kids. It doesn't matter how our delicates get folded. They're only going under our skinny jeans or in our underwear drawer. And don't be a control freak who doesn't trust anyone. It creates incredibly negative energy and just makes you look like a martyr—no one likes a martyr. Trust me, I had to resist all those urges pretty hard when my girls were young. And it wasn't easy. But I did it so they could ultimately be more independent. And they are.

Because when we don't teach our kids to be independent and to take ownership of the things in their little world (things like their toys and their clothes and their room), then they become entitled. And those kinds of kids are gross. I'm sorry, but they are . They expect everything to be done for them, and they complain when it's not.

I used to see those types of kids every day when I taught in the classroom. Kids like this one little girl who never liked to clean up her workspace after we did an activity. Religiously, she'd finish her little cutting or gluing project and just get up from the table and walk away, leaving her work area a total disaster and expecting the other kids working at the table to clean up after her.

And I remember the first time she did it, too, because I called her over to clean up her mess and she just looked at me and said, "But why? They're doing it for me," pointing at the other kids around the table. It wasn't until I asked her what she did when she was at home and made a mess that I figured it out . . . her mom was always cleaning up after her. And there it was: she wasn't being held accountable.

Our kids need to be kids, above all. They work hard when they're young, even though it's a different type of work and a different sort of pace. And we need to remember that. That's why it can be tricky for us to know how much responsibility to put on them and when. Especially since school and sleep and downtime are such priorities. But like I've said, kids can bear more weight than we realize—*than they realize*. And, most importantly, they almost always rise to the occasion, whatever that occasion is. Which means we need to challenge them, even early on. Because if we don't, then they won't have the desire to challenge themselves. And you'll end up with a twenty-seven-year-old deadbeat for a kid living in your basement. Not cool.

Myth #14

Myth: Possession is nine-tenths of the law.

Reality: Sharing makes the world go 'round.

Sometimes we have to share. We just do. And not because we necessarily want to (like giving up the really big flowers on the delish-looking slice of birthday cake), or even because we should (like giving up our seat to the pregnant lady on the train), but simply because it's what people need to do to get along. Unfortunately, though, not everyone does it well. And teaching it to our kids can be super stressful. But it's a way more important life skill than most of us realize—a critical skill that our kids have to learn whether they want to or not.

Now, the average person can usually suck it up and share, even if it isn't our first choice. But we're adults, so most of us have learned the importance and the necessity of sharing. We get that it's just an obligatory people skill. Toss a couple of young, immature kids into the mix who are both after the same basketball or hula hoop and all bets are off. Then it's a complete free-for-all. That's because learning to part with things, especially things we like or enjoy, isn't easy. And it's especially challenging for kids.

So like we do with every other life skill our kids have to learn, we hammer at them to get comfortable with sharing because it's something they're going to have to be able to do throughout their life. And we start early because there's always the potential for hair-pulling or shoving or meltdowns when you put kids together in any given situation but that potential explodes when one of them wants what the other one has. So the sooner we teach them that sharing is just a necessary part of life, the better.

Of course we all expect toddlers to be awful at parting with stuff because toddlers are egocentric, selfish little people. It's a fact. And any of us who've ever had a toddler knows it. But the expectation is that, eventually, our greedy little guys who hate to hand stuff over will evolve into generous, mature preschoolers and adolescents who are happy to share. The problem is, that doesn't always happen quite as soon and quite as easily as we'd all like. And the reason is because, to little kids, the word *sharing* and the concept behind it is meaningless. They don't see any good reason why they need to give up their dolls or their toys or give their friend a turn on the swing. At least not right away.

I mean, sure, our kids do ultimately learn that they have to share or let other people have a chance using their stuff, but it certainly doesn't happen overnight. Even though we desperately wish it would. Sharing is very much a learned skill. It's one of those abilities that needs to be taught and reinforced and retaught and re-reinforced for what seems like forever. Which is why we have to be tireless in our efforts to drill the concept into their little brains.

Now, technically speaking, kids don't really even have a shot at grasping the concept of sharing until they're around five.[14] This is according to the professionals at Parents.com. Which, coincidentally, is almost the exact time when they start school and start interacting regularly with other nonsharers. (Great timing.) Not to worry, though; kids are pretty moldable, as a general rule. A lot like Play-Doh, I've found. We just have to keep squishing them into the shape we want, and, eventually, they harden that way.

We also have to get creative when we're teaching our kids these skills. Kind of like how we have to get creative when we sneak veggies into our kid's lunches. You know, how we grind them up so they're unrecognizable and then camouflage them as other things so our kids can't detect them.

And we have to do the same thing when we teach them good people skills, too. We have to make a game out of it so they don't realize we're actually teaching them a valuable life skill. Like keeping a tally of how many doors they hold open for people or how many times they say "please" and "thank you" or how often they clear the dishes at home or how many times they share their toys during a playdate. And then we celebrate those moments with a little praise and recognition and maybe a Blow Pop, just like we do when they swallow down a big forkful of spinach. Because it's good for them, and we want them to remember.

Unfortunately, though, not everybody has the aptitude for sharing. And there are plenty of people—kids and grown-ups—who just can't do it, no matter how much they're taught that they should. But as a mom, seeing those types of people only strengthens my resolve to ensure that I get the point across with my own kids. And it should be the same for you.

Seeing little kids struggle with sharing is pretty common and expected. It's just one part of the learning process. But we've all seen those adults who completely lack the capacity to share, and those people drive me nuts. Those are the people I just want to grab by the shoulders and shake vigorously until they get it. (But since I'm a lover, not a fighter, I don't.) Like the guy at the mall who whizzes into the parking spot you've been patiently idling in front of for five minutes, even though there are dozens of spaces in the next aisle. Or the friends who refuse to compromise on where you go out to eat. Or the coworker who you carpool with that's consistently late. Or the woman at the office who constantly talks about herself and has never once asked about you. Or your husband who won't share the remote (Not you, Dave; don't worry!). And it's a real disappointment, especially when you see that kind of behavior from an adult.

I mean, we more or less expect it from kids, because kids are naturally territorial. They also get easily attached to stuff, which makes it even tougher for them to learn how to play cooperatively. Because they're convinced that having their friend's Luke Skywalker action figure is the *only* thing on the planet that will make them happy. That, and they completely lack the ability when they're young to part with anything. But we're the adults, so modeling good behavior is entirely up to us. And we need to get it right. For our kids' sakes.

So when my girls were young, like super-impressionable kindergarten age, I used to purposely let Dave have the remote once in a while when we were watching TV with the girls. Now, make no mistake; I really didn't want to give up watching the Food Network, but I did it anyway as a carefully orchestrated parenting move to model good behavior for my kids. And I did stuff like that all the time. Like I'd be savagely craving Italian for dinner, but I'd still openly ask everyone in my family where *they* wanted to eat. Or I'd almost always give my girls free rein over the music they listened to in the car, as painful as that was (there's only so much *Top 40 Countdown* a human being can take). It was the easy, relatively small stuff like that that helped subtly reinforce the fact that Dave and I knew how to share too. And while that didn't keep my kids from screwing up and not sharing sometimes, I think it definitely helped strengthen my argument that everyone needs to be able to do it. Because Dave and I were walking the walk ourselves every chance we got.

But no parenting technique is foolproof, and my kids tended to forget certain rules of engagement at least as often as they would remember them. And the sharing rule was a biggie for forgetting. Which is why so many interactions between my girls would predictably end up with one of them crying or whining because the other one wouldn't let her lie on the living room couch to watch TV. Or they couldn't give their sister a turn sitting in the front seat of the car. Or one of them was hogging all the beach toys. It's unavoidable. But that's just the road we have to follow when we have kids. We have to absorb the bumps and chunks of broken asphalt until the road smooths out a little and the ride becomes a little easier. Because it does. It just takes about ninety thousand miles worth of travel to get there.

See, sharing is just another one of those ethical, moral lessons kids need a while to learn to digest. And since I'm not about blowing sunshine, I'm being honest that it's a constant challenge. We're always sharing stuff, to varying degrees—stuff like our space or our time or our friends or our opinions—so we have to become adept at being able to do it or we're setting ourselves up for a rough ride if we plan on interacting with other people throughout our lifetime. And the sooner we get our kids comfortable with the idea, the better off everyone will be.

So how do we help? How do we handle it when our kid won't hand over the Barbie or share the bowl of grapes or give another kid a turn at bat? Well, we do exactly what we do when we teach them any life skill—we clarify why it's important and then we set the expectation. We don't ever force them to share, because kids inherently reject anything we force them to do. So instead, we make sharing appealing by promoting its benefits, like how good it will make them or the people they're sharing with feel. But more than that, if they share, it'll motivate other kids to share with them. We encourage them to do it every chance we get. And we guide them in knowing when it's appropriate to share and when they really don't have to. That's how we make it happen.

We use tricks like timers that divide up the time fairly, and if our kids just can't get there on their own, then we time-out the thing that they can't part with. (Don't time-out the kid; just remove the thing that they're having trouble giving up from the equation.) Then we explain that until everyone can learn how to take turns, it's off limits. We keep it all positive. And we model *all* of that ourselves and make sure our kids see us doing it so that we make that modeling into teachable moments.

The truth is, having something that someone else wants is a powerful position to be in, and kids pick up on that pretty early on in their lives. That's why we have to cultivate an environment where our kids are used to and comfortable with sharing. Because if our daughter can't let Suzie have a turn with her American Girl doll in the second grade, then she's not going to learn how to work or live or collaborate with other people later on in life. That's just the harsh truth.

Look, in the beginning, letting people use our stuff or have what we want is painful. Hell, it's painful at times even when we're adults. But letting someone have a turn with something doesn't mean we're losing it forever. It's not a permanent give-away. It's usually a back and forth. At least in theory. Which is the key factor that we always have to stress with our kids. Over and over and over.

At the same time, though (and I know this sounds kind of counterintuitive), kids shouldn't be expected to share *every-thing*. It's actually OK for certain special things to be reserved just for them. (Although if my girls had their way, every single solitary possession they had growing up would fall under that category just as a loophole.) But in all fairness, it really is a good thing to have a handful of special toys or dolls or pieces of clothing that are ours and ours alone. And the reason I believe that is because it's a respect thing. It's important to recognize that even if we live in a family environment, where things are regularly borrowed and shared, we're allowed to preserve a little bit of ownership over a few special things. It's called having boundaries, and to a degree, that's OK. Especially with siblings. Because even if most things are communal, not everything needs to be. Everyone deserves to have a little individuality and personal space that's reserved for just them.

For those of you raising an only child, though: I know you're especially worried right now about whether or not your kid will grow up knowing how to share. Because without another child to have to learn to share with, it's natural to wonder how an only child will learn to interact when other kids are thrown into the mix. And I know this because I was that only child. I was the kid who grew up having carte blanche over everything in my house because there was no competition.

I know, from plenty of conversations over the years with my mom, that she was consciously aware of the potential for me to grow up into a spoiled little brat. Because, let's be honest, only children do, by default, have that rep. Most people hear *only child* and they automatically think of qualities like *overindulged, self-centered,* and *obnoxious.* Trust me, over the course of my lifetime, I've had countless people tell me how shocked they were to find out that I was an only child. They were surprised because I just never behaved like the stereotypical only child. I was always really comfortable sharing; I was always very sensitive of other peoples' feelings; I was a team player. But that's how I was raised.

Even though I didn't have to jockey for my mom's or dad's

attention growing up or fight with a brother for the remote or lend a sister my favorite hoodie, I still learned, very early on, that it wasn't all about me. My parents taught me to always consider the people around me and act accordingly, because we live in a big world where everybody has to get along and no one cares if you were raised with or without siblings. All people care about is that you know how to behave like a rational, kind, considerate human being.

As far as I'm concerned, traits like thoughtfulness aren't genetic. Being considerate of others is something we learn. And we learn it from the top down. Parents set the tone at home. In every home. We set it every step of the way. And I don't care where someone grew up or what they have or don't have; the kind of genetic predisposition a kid has is a direct result of the environment *we* create.

So if we raise a kid with an elitist or entitled or snotty attitude who doesn't know how to share and be considerate of other people, then we should naturally assume that our kids learned that from somewhere. Duh. And at that point, we should be looking squarely in the mirror, because that's where it's coming from.

If we don't stress that our kids have to take turns, then they'll never pass the ball. If we don't stress that our kids have to be kind, then they'll be little snots around everyone else. If we don't stress that our kids need to include everyone, then they'll be snobs. It's that simple.

I can't even put an accurate number on how many entitled kids I've seen come through my school over the years. But I *can* tell you from personal interactions with them and their parents that they were little carbon copies of their moms and dads—rude and self-absorbed and bossy. They were the kids who demanded all the new crayons in art class or threw a fit when they struck out at Wiffle ball or when they couldn't sit next to their best friend at lunch. I had kids so bad at sharing that they literally couldn't handle it when other kids got to read out loud in circle time. Selfishness takes on many forms.

That's why it's so critical that we teach our kids to be considerate and empathetic since there are *always* going to be other people who want and need the same things we do. Maybe even at the exact same second that we need it. And by teaching our kids to give up pole position in the sandbox, just because someone else might like that spot, we're actually helping them cultivate a spirit of generosity. And that can carry a person a long, long way in their lifetime.

So in the spirit of setting a strong example for our kids, we have to make a steady, concerted effort to hand over the clicker or share the car radio or divvy up the chores around the house, because whether we realize it or not, our kids are watching. They're watching everything we do and listening to everything we say, and they're imitating. Heavily. And since we're the ones they look to first as role models for good behavior, we have to be on point with this stuff all the time. Like 24/7. Because crappy kid sharers come from one place . . . crappy parent sharers.

Myth #15

Myth: My child is behind the eight ball, and she'll never catch up.

Reality: Our kids don't all learn how to ride a bike on the same day.

As parents, we do a lot of comparing of our kids, both to their own siblings (if they have them) and to the kids around them. Especially once they hit school age. We intentionally and unintentionally measure them against their brothers or sisters and other kids because we just can't help ourselves. We're curious about how other kids are growing and maturing and adapting, and we want to ensure that our own kids are staying on track with their peers. And yeah, on some level, we're also a little competitive. *Can't have Jen's kid swimming without a swim bubble before my kid!*

I mean, how many times have you said to yourself, *Why isn't my kid reading yet? How can the Smith kid possibly be reading Level 5 books already?! Why can't my daughter ride a two-wheeler? How come my son can't throw to first base? Why isn't my kid as tall as the other kids in his class?* And I get it, because *I've been that mom*, thinking those exact same thoughts. It's impossible not to. And anyone who says they haven't is flat out lying. But what we absolutely can never become is the mom or dad who calls our kid out to her face for not being as fast or as smart or as strong as all the other kids. That's like the cardinal sin of parenting.

It's one thing to talk privately to our husband or wife about concerns we have about our son or daughter's social or emotional or academic progress; that's cool. Being aware of and in tune with where our kids are at is good parenting. That's what we're supposed to do. But start doing that in front of the *actual* kid, and that becomes totally uncool. Then you're sending a very clear-cut message to your child that it's not OK for them to develop at a speed that's comfortable for them. Then you're kicking them directly in the bull's-eye of their self-esteem, which says that they're not measuring up.

We all want the best for our kids. Obviously. We all want them to succeed and thrive and excel, but they're not going to do that according to someone else's pace. They're going to do it only when they're ready. And to try to force it only creates animosity between you and them. To set unfair expectations according to how other kids develop is just unrealistic and sets an awful precedent. Which is exactly why we need to embrace our kids exactly where they are. We need to let them feel our support and our patience, because when they know they have that, that's exactly when they start to blossom. And when they think they don't, that's when they implode. It's when they start paying too much attention to what everyone around them is doing that the big-time inferiority complex usually surfaces.

Being in the school system for so long, I saw a disturbing number of parents shooting down their kids for not making the varsity team or high honor roll or getting MVP. And it was disgusting. I've had kids as young as first graders admit to me that they thought their dad liked their older brother better than them because the brother could hit the ball farther. I also know plenty of siblings who were openly compared against each other—friends of my own kids. These were parents who made no secret of the fact that they expected their younger child to play the same sport, at the same level, as their sister. Whether they were into the sport or not. So in addition to creating performance anxiety in their kid, they also forged a rivalry between siblings that may not ever have been there to begin with.

Like the dad I bumped into at the park one day when my girls were still young. He had played college football and felt the need to unload on me how inadequate he felt because his son sucked at Pop Warner football. He said his daughter could play better. He just couldn't let it go. And all I could think of was, *Poor kid, to live in that shadow.* Or the gymnastics mom I used to sit next to at tumbling who would complain about her daughter not being able to do a cartwheel. Made her daughter feel horrible in front of all the other girls, not to mention the other moms. She criticized her every time the girl tumbled by. It was awful to hear, but imagine what it must've felt like to be her daughter. No big surprise that the little girl didn't stick with gymnastics.

It's sad, really, that so many parents are more hung up on their kids performing well, or better than their peers, than they are concerned with their kids being truly happy. And that's because, unfortunately, a lot of parents are competitive and see their kids as a reflection of themselves. If they were captain of the basketball team when they were young, they expect their kid to play hoops and to be good at it. So when their kids don't perform well, they take it as a personal slam—almost like they've failed somehow as a parent.

We as grown-ups need to realize that our kids pick up on our approval as much as our disapproval. Disapproval even more, I think. Which is why we need to celebrate their strengths and help support their weaknesses. We need to empower them to take their time and work hard at what they love. And we need to be OK when our thing isn't their thing.

In a nutshell, we all need to relax. Our kids are OK whether they can hit the ball as far as their friends can or not. They're OK if they don't learn how to tread water on the same day that all the other kids do. They're OK if they aren't drawing masterpieces in the third grade.

You've heard of late bloomers, right? Well, my oldest was one, and she's doing just fine. Better than fine, actually. Not to brag, but . . . she made the dean's list her freshman year of college and is successfully involved with more extracurricular activities than our whole family combined. And I'm telling you this for a very specific reason. Because at our first parent-teacher conference, when Riley was in preschool, her teacher told us to consider holding her back. Apparently, she did everything on what they called "Riley Time" and didn't always want to stop doing whatever she was doing when it was time for everyone to transition. Pretty normal for a four-year-old, but the concern was that she would fall behind.

And Dave and I went back and forth about what to do, worried that if we didn't hold her back, we'd be setting her up to fail further down the line. But, ultimately, we took a step back and decided not to have her repeat preschool. We felt, at the time, that everyone blossoms at different times and that she barely had one foot in the door at school yet, so we didn't judge where she was at too prematurely. And, man, were we glad we let her move on. Because, eventually, she found her mojo.

Worth mentioning, too: Riley couldn't draw more than a stick figure until she was in the eighth grade. But since she had no interest in going to art school, we didn't put too much emphasis on her being able to draw a still life as well as the other kids. Instead, we let her focus on playing the violin and learning how to ski, and eventually, she caught up. When the desire was there, she caught up. And that's key. When our kids start discovering the things that inspire them, they usually turn on the jets and really start moving. She also played soccer from the time she was in kindergarten all the way up to high school. Loved the sport. Loved that Dave coached her. Loved that she got to run around every day on a big field with her friends. Never scored a goal in a regular-season game in her entire career as a player. But that didn't hold her back. That didn't impact her. Instead, when she got to high school, she decided to try something new. Decided to try running cross country just to be part of a team.

And wouldn't you know, the kid who ran a ten-minute mile her freshman year became captain of the cross country team her senior year and walked off as a six-minute miler.

Oh yeah, and when she was halfway through the eighth grade, one of Riley's artsy friends taught her the basics of drawing portraits, and that changed everything for her. Something clicked, and this artist that none of us knew was inside her emerged. So much so that she was inducted as a member of the National Art Honor Society her senior year of high school. I mean, who knew? More proof that sometimes it's just about timing. Especially with kids.

And that's the thing. It's sometimes hard to distinguish between a kid who's falling behind and a kid who just hasn't found her groove yet. Because in a lot of cases, our kids just haven't found their rhythm, so it's a challenge for us to know when there's a legitimate problem and when they're just not interested in something. That's why we have to be diligent, faithful observers, ever watching.

In our role as our kids' moms and dads, one of our primary jobs is to encourage them to pursue what inspires them and teach them not to care about keeping up with the people around them. We're supposed to push them to follow their own unique path and send a consistent message that *they* get to decide what they like and, just as important, that their best is enough. Because, believe me, as a soccer mom, I watched plenty of miserable little kids running up and down the field complaining about how much they hated soccer. All they wanted to do was swim or play basketball or ice skate. But for whatever reason, their parents pushed soccer.

Now, don't misunderstand: I'm not suggesting that our six- and seven-year-olds get to drive the bus and call all the shots in terms of what they do. They're still just kids who need a gentle kick in the behind most of the time. But what I am saying is that at some point, after we've done our job exposing them to different things and encouraging them to mix it up, we should respect them if they don't make a love connection with a particular sport or activity. We need to teach them to honor the commitment they make to their team or group, but after that's over, if they're still not feeling the love, they can try something else.

Once we put our kid in the mix with a whole bunch of other kids, that natural inclination to compare all of them kicks in. So do yourself a favor and don't be too freaked out if you're doing it, because we all do it, to some degree.

You've heard the corny old expression *The grass is always greener on the other side of the fence*, right? Well, that expression was born for a reason. It started because, historically, people compared themselves to other people. It's just human nature.

We do it to learn more about ourselves as people—who we are, who we want to be, what we like and don't like. But there's a huge difference between comparing and judging, especially where our kids are concerned.

OK, I know, we want to ensure that our kids are keeping up with their peers and not getting too far behind the eight ball. That's normal. And wanting that doesn't make us bad parents. We just have to remember that kids—all kids—develop different skills at different paces and at different times. And that's OK. Focus on my words . . . *that's OK*.

I've watched dads scream at their sons for not getting to the ball fast enough and heard moms belittle their daughters for letting in a goal *that the other goalie could've stopped.* And every time I see it, it makes me ill, because it makes the kids feel like inadequate losers.

With Dave as a soccer coach for over twenty seasons and me coaching cross country since 2012, we've both seen our share of kids getting reamed by their parents for not scoring enough points or running fast enough or trying hard enough. And trust me, it doesn't get any easier to see each time we're confronted with it. We need to do ourselves and our kids a favor and not get too hung up on where everybody's at on the learning curve. Because, in most cases, they all get to where they're supposed to be eventually. Just at a slightly different pace. But they most definitely won't get there through intimidation and bullying.

It's just common sense that we shouldn't be comparing our kids to anyone—and certainly not to their face. It's counterproductive and hurtful. And it leaves an indelible mark. That's because doing too much comparing only gives our kids an inferiority complex, and that's a pretty heavy weight to bear as a kid. Because when a little girl feels inadequate, it's almost inevitable that she'll become a young adult who feels insecure and then, ultimately, a self-doubting grown-up. And we all know that hollow feeling of thinking we don't measure up. It can wreck us.

Too many parents worry about looking bad if their kids aren't performing at the same level as the kids around them. I remember one of my girlfriends almost throwing up in her mouth when she heard my daughter Riley (five at the time) reading beginner reading books. She was in a frenzy over the fact that her daughter, who was a little older than Riley, wasn't stringing words together yet. And she just couldn't let it go. She wanted to get her daughter tested for a learning disability, stat, just because her daughter wasn't at the exact same reading level as my kid. Caaa-ray-zeee! And she didn't hold back saying any of that in front of her daughter, who was frustrated enough because she couldn't read.

Needless to say, some of the other moms and I had to have a little intervention to stop her from hurtling off the deep end and running straight to the Special Ed Chair at the school department. We reminded her that if her daughter is a little ahead or even a little behind with some skills, it's perfectly normal. And that with the right kind of support and nurturing at home and in the classroom, most kids will catch up to where they're supposed to be. (Just as a point of fact, that same girl graduated high school with my daughter a couple of years ago and went on to an Ivy League school. Just sayin'.)

Unfortunately, the underlying problem with a lot of parents is that they take it personally if their child is a little behind. Like they're actually embarrassed that their son can't drain a free throw or draw a house that looks like a house. Or that their daughter can't hula hoop like the other girls. And when our kids are constantly being compared to other kids, that insecurity eventually has an impact—and not the good kind.

Being able to "measure" our kids against other kids their age is a healthy thing when it helps us keep track of the age-appropriate stages our kids are cycling through. But it's a very bad thing when it turns from casual observation into nitpicking and criticism.

The fact is, an awful lot of growth happens between the ages of five and eight. A lot. But again, not all kids will start doing the same things at the same time or at the same speed. All. Kids. Are. Different. Remember that, and don't crucify yourself if your kid can't pump as high as all the other kids can on the swings.

It's only when *we* let go of the idea that our kids need to do certain things at certain times that our kids can do the same. They need to know that we're OK with them hitting their stride at their own pace. Because that's when our kids are free to develop without unfair expectations.

Because today's parents are so hyperfocused on making sure that their kids excel at everything, it's tricky to know when to pull back and let them grow at their own pace and when to push. And that's got a lot of us in knots, because no one wants to watch their kid get lapped by everyone around them. As a result, parents everywhere are micromanaging their kids and putting too much pressure on them to outperform their peers, whether our kids are up for it or not. With so many different developmental milestones to check off, both in and out of school, a lot of parents are ignoring where their kids are really at developmentally and focusing instead on where they think they ought to be to measure up.

We're the first teachers our kids ever have, so if we put unreasonable expectations on them to do things before they're ready, we're setting them up for failure down the line. If we compare them to everyone around them, we're ensuring they develop an inferiority complex. And if we judge them too harshly for not being able to keep up, we're gonna crush their self-esteem. So it's up to us to adapt to their pace. Even though we often think we know what's best for them. And since we don't get an owner's manual when our kids are born, learning what their pace is is more or less trial by fire.

Remember, some kids jump straight to walking and never crawl. Some kids read in kindergarten; some don't. Some kids potty train in one shot; others just keep pooping in their pants for weeks. But they *do* get there. And since the pace that they get there is already imprinted on their DNA from the get-go, we need to quit comparing them and start embracing them. They'll thank you for it later—I promise.

Myth #16

Myth: IQ is more important than EQ.

Reality: EQ is more important than IQ.

As parents, we wish for a long list of things when we raise our kids. We pray for them to have good health and a good temperament and good social skills. We want them to be smart and well-adjusted and kind and instinctively know how to keep their rooms clean, among so many other things. But when you dissect the list carefully, two things stand out as must-haves, at least for me—EQ (Emotional Quotient) and IQ (Intelligence Quotient).

Psychcentral.com says EQ "is the ability to identify, use, understand, and manage emotions in an effective and positive way. A high EQ helps us communicate better, reduce our anxiety and stress, defuse conflicts, improve our relationships, empathize with others, and effectively overcome challenges.

Our emotional intelligence affects the quality of our lives because it influences our behavior and relationships."[15]

So what I don't get is that if our EQ enables us to do all those things, why isn't growing our kids' EQs considered a priority across the board—especially since IQ does none of those things?

Now, it's a given that both are invaluable qualities that can, in large part, make or break our kids' future. The question is, though: is one more important than the other? And is it the one we've all been trained to expect?

I know we were all taught when we were young that education is everything. *Pay attention in school; get good grades. That's how you'll make something of yourself.* That a good education would propel us toward a bright future. And to a huge degree, that's true. But what I've also learned as a mom is that there are a lot more critical traits associated with raising a solid kid than we realize. And being book smart is only one. Funny, too, but it may not even be the most important one.

In my opinion, our EQ is one of the *most* crucial and underrated strengths we can develop. I mean, what good is it having a card-holding Mensa member for a kid if they can't look someone in the eye while they're talking? Or if they don't have the ability to be empathetic with people? Or if they can't be a good friend? Or if they lack the capacity to care about someone else's feelings? Because all of those things matter. They matter a lot. Some may say they matter the most. I certainly do. But I think it's not until we raise kids ourselves that we realize how much a strong EQ really matters in life.

And Travis Bradberry, author of *Emotional Intelligence 2.0* and a contributing writer at Forbes.com, agrees. According to

Bradberry, "our emotional intelligence is the foundation for a host of critical skills—it impacts most everything you say and do each day. Emotional intelligence is the single biggest predictor of performance in the workplace and the strongest driver of leadership and personal excellence."[16]

Raising two of my own daughters and watching them grow and interact with other people along the way, I've come to realize the value of having kids who can relate with the people around them and read social cues. Kids who can express themselves well and be in touch with their feelings and actually emote. Kids who know how to adapt to the people and situations around them. Because I've seen the other side.

I've seen kids who couldn't control their emotions, not because they had behavioral issues but because they just lacked a healthy emotional infrastructure. I've dealt with kids who were incapable of making emotional connections with other kids because they were just clueless about other people's feelings. I've watched kids lose friend after friend because they just couldn't keep their emotions in check. They'd scream at someone or be overly critical or toss out an insult without thinking twice. And even though these kids might score well on tests and be "smart" according to academic standards, they're oblivious to how their actions affect the people around them.

Look, I know that in a perfect world, we'd all love to raise a son or a daughter with the full monty—a high EQ and an equally high IQ. We'd all love for our kids to be book smart and have good social skills, a strong sense of responsibility, good judgment, and a big heart. That's the ultimate goal. But no one's perfect, and there's no such thing as the perfect child. Realistically, most people end up being a combo of all those things.

Now that I have the perspective of being a parent for almost twenty years, I can honestly say that I don't feel like enough emphasis has been put on the EQ side of our kids' growth and development, on raising kids who are emotionally well-balanced and secure.

Sure, a person's IQ measures their raw intelligence. But it's pretty much just based on one-dimensional test scores. On being able to interpret and process and regurgitate what we read in books or what we learn from teachers. Our EQ, though, is our sense of street smarts. It's being able to use our common sense to navigate the world around us. And—I don't know, maybe it's just me—but I kinda think that might trump just about everything else.

Raising a kid with a solid EQ means they have what's called *situational awareness*, which, in simple terms, means that they know what's going on around them and can adapt to changes in their environment like a boss. It's a top-tier life skill, as far as I'm concerned.

And I feel so strongly about EQ being such an important quality that if I could choose to have a child with only one of the quotients, I'd pick EQ. No contest.

See, according to *Forbes* online, IQ tests are used as an indicator of logical reasoning ability and technical intelligence, i.e., how much information we can assimilate. On the flip side are the EQ tests that measure our awareness of our own feelings and the feelings of others. They rate how we regulate these feelings in ourselves and other people, how we use emotions that are appropriate to a situation, self-motivation, and our ability to build relationships.[17] And that's a pretty big deal in the grand scheme of life.

What I'm suggesting is that, as parents, we learn early on to focus on the whole child, not just on the one who's going to need to apply to college somewhere down the line. Because while being a high academic achiever will definitely open lots of doors for our kids later on in life, it won't ensure that those doors stay open.

Our kids need good interpersonal skills and communication skills to be successful in life, too. In high school and college and beyond. They need to be critical thinkers and have the ability to be nimble and to ask questions and to read people and situations. They need to be able to multitask and manage their time and take criticism and accept failure. They need to know how to do a lot.

We've all heard stories about the Doogie Howser–like kids who weren't being academically challenged in their age-appropriate grade so their parents skipped them ahead so they wouldn't be bored. Well, I've seen the other side of that decision to push them forward just based on test scores and academics regardless of whether or not they were ready emotionally. And I've gotta say, I don't agree with it. The reason is simply that just because they might be ready one way doesn't mean they're ready in all the ways that count. Just because they can keep up with college kids on paper doesn't mean that they're ready for all the other aspects of college. Like living on their own and using good judgment and budgeting their time and resisting temptation and having no one there to tell them when it's bedtime.

I've seen the fifteen-year-old kid graduate from high school and go straight on to college when he was barely hitting puberty. It happened to a boy in Libby's class. And while I have no

idea how he acclimated to college life at that age, I can't imagine it was a seamless transition considering he was thrown into
an adult world way before he was an actual adult. I mean, how
can a kid that age possibly connect with his peers when they're
in such vastly different places physically and emotionally? A
fifteen-year-old kid is hardly ready to live on his own with a
bunch of eighteen- to twenty-two-year-olds and shouldn't be
expected to thrive just because he got a perfect score on his
SATs. Especially in an environment that relies heavily on street
smarts and common sense to be successful.

I'm using this as an example for the simple reason that we
have to acknowledge, when our kids are still young, that even
though we live in a culture that's hyperfocused on academic
excellence, it's not the only thing that's important as we raise
them.

I just think that when the motivation to see our kids succeed
intellectually outweighs the desire to see them thrive emotionally, we're setting ourselves (and them) up for problems. That's
because it takes way more than just book smarts to be successful. Kids need the total package of academic and social and
emotional and physical maturity to be able to make it. We can't
just hammer at them about test scores and report card grades.
They need to know that there's more to life than being able to
score well on standardized tests. Because being the smartest
person in the room doesn't matter if no one likes you because
you can't relate to anyone.

Look, with a daughter in high school and another one in
college, I'm intimately aware of how much grades and standardized test scores matter. Getting into a good college largely
depends on them. But don't fall into the trap that so many of

us are prone to where the only thing we care about (or act like we care about) are grades. Because while they are important for obvious reasons, they're not the end-all-be-all. There are other factors in play here, and we need to focus our attention on those things too. Things like strong self-image, and the ability to play well with other kids, and knowing how and when to listen and how to stay in control when we're on the edge. Because if our kids think that the only thing we care about is the grade on a paper or whether or not they make the honor roll, then we're sending a damaging message that could have a pretty catastrophic impact as they get older.

I've seen the other side of that parent pressure up close, and it's a pretty ugly thing to watch. Working for so many years around kids, I saw how constant pressure to perform affected kids in some pretty profound ways, like causing eating disorders, anxiety, sleep disorders, and depression. And the kids I'm talking about weren't even middle school or high school kids. They were elementary school kids.

I can't tell you how many grammar school parents I've encountered who were neurotic at the end of every quarter when it was time for report cards to be distributed. And those report cards don't even have traditional letter grades! You'd have thought their kids were in their senior year of high school and their Ivy League acceptances depended on what was on that paper.

Instead of being concerned that their kid got a *Needs Improvement* on *Follows Class Rules* or *Works Cooperatively* or *Shows Respect for Others*, all those parents cared about was that their kid got a four out of four in *Number Sense* or *Algebra and Functions*. And they'd threaten their kids with consequences or punishments if the next report card wasn't stellar.

The problem is, putting that kind of pressure on our kids can backfire. Badly. I saw countless kids implode because they were afraid of failing a third-grade spelling test. I had kids cry to me that their mom was going to yell at them if they didn't get a good grade on a math test. I've had kids go to the nurse's office, day after day, with a "stomachache" that was actually just stress manifested as real pain. All because their moms and dads thought that grades were the most important thing. And that's sad, because they're not.

For me, though, those *Social Skills* and *Listening and Speaking* sections were always where my eyes went when I ripped into that envelope every quarter. Because to my husband and me, those were the things that mattered most. Knowing that our daughters could relate to their peers and treat their teacher with respect was of paramount importance to us. And we told our girls that's what mattered the most.

From the time they understood what grades and report cards were, we told our girls that we expected their best effort in school—whether that effort resulted in straight As or straight Cs. Because, in the end, not everything comes easily to every-one. We all learn in different ways and to different degrees. But effort is effort. And a strong work ethic can compensate a lot for weaknesses in other areas, like book smarts.

In my case, I was the kid who didn't have a natural apti-tude for learning flat, one-dimensional stuff. I was the visual kid, the one who needed pictures and hands-on interactions with the material I was learning in order to make it stick. I was not a naturally brainy kid, like a lot of my friends. I struggled to learn dates and concepts and formulas and always felt like I spent twice the amount of time everybody else did trying to be successful academically.

But I worked hard. Really, really hard. And I was organized. I was the kid who stayed after school for help and did the extra credit and threw my hand up every time my teacher asked a question. And to this day, I believe it's those things that carried me through. Being diligent made all the difference for me in terms of being able to stay with the pack and not fall behind. Those were my advantages. And I exploited them as much as I possibly could.

See, I figured out early on that it was going to have to be my people and organizational skills and drive that would sustain me. Not my raw IQ. And so far, so good. That's why, personally, I think that having a high IQ is grossly overrated in terms of it being the key to a successful life.

As a kid who almost always tested poorly on any kind of standardized test, I've always felt strongly that academics alone just aren't a true indicator of a person's ability or potential. There are *so* many other facets to our personalities that I don't think it's fair to assume that a transcript full of grades is more important to a person's overall success than their ability to relate well with people or their ability to be kind or listen to a friend.

Now, don't get me wrong; of course there's a part of me that would love to have an IQ of 140 and have a glossy Mensa membership card in my wallet. But when it really comes down to it, that intelligence quotient is not what I really think we need the most to be successful in life. It's important, no doubt, but when we really break it down, having a high IQ offers absolutely no guarantee that we'll lead a successful life. And while I totally recognize that it opens certain doors that may otherwise have stayed closed, a high IQ is no guarantee that you'll be able to keep your high-profile, high-paying job.

I mean, if you can't relate with people or build and maintain relationships, then you won't be in your sweet new job for very long. Because people won't like you, and you'll probably get fired. And that's because without the vital people skills you need to function in the mainstream, you'll never be able to successfully collaborate. Remember, there's no "i" in "team" for a reason.

According to a Carnegie Institute of Technology study, eighty-five percent of a person's financial success is due to skills in human engineering, which includes your personality and your ability to communicate, negotiate, and lead. And, shockingly, only fifteen percent is due to technical knowledge.[18] Kinda makes you think, doesn't it? Kinda gives what I'm talking about a little more credence, doesn't it? Or, at the very least, gives you something to think about.

With our girls, we always emphasized that it's their effort that matters most. Sure, we push them to work hard and aim as high as they can, and sometimes that doesn't translate to an A or a perfect score. Sometimes their academic best is just going to be mediocre, but that doesn't mean that they've failed. It just means that their strengths lie elsewhere. And it's up to us to empower them with the emotional strength to find them.

Myth #17

Myth: Saying "No" to my kids makes me a horrible parent.

Reality: We have to say "No" to our kids.

From the time our kids are little, they want what other kids around them have. No big surprise there. And the last word in the English language that they ever seem to accept is *No*.

As soon as they learn how to pilot their chubby little hands, they're reaching for everything. They're grabbing toys away from their friends, throwing fits, and whining incessantly for us to get them the same thing. And the whining evolves very quickly into grunting for those things, which develops even quicker into flat-out demanding them. Sometimes to the point where it feels like their first real words are *I want*. And even though that never really ends (sorry), they do usually develop a little perspective once they're older and more mature (I say again, *usually*). It's the time in between that's the tricky part.

It's when our kids are young that we have to get really comfortable using the word *no*. Like really, really comfortable. Because if we don't pump those brakes early, we run the risk of sliding, headfirst, into a world of spoiled brattiness. And I feel pretty confident you can imagine what that's like.

Now why is it that kids always want the stuff other kids have? And why can't they ever take no for an answer? (Rhetorical questions, I know.) Well, it's because (a) somebody else has it, and (b) they're just not capable of understanding much of anything yet in the way of real limits.

We see it in playgroups, during playdates, and with brothers and sisters. It's a constant issue when our kids are young, an issue that causes huge amounts of stress and anxiety for us and for them. And even though most of us do everything in our power to reason with our kids when they just *have* to have something, a five- or six-year-old has little to no capacity for sustained rational behavior. So it's basically pointless.

Over the years, I've watched little kids go at it with their parents in every public place you can think of, arguing with them because they were just handed a clear and decisive "no." The problem was, after time, the parents caved because the kid was unrelenting. But *we're* the parents. We're the ones who are supposed to have the mental toughness to combat a whiny seven-year-old. Because, you know, they're seven and we still have the ability, as long as we're taller, to pick them up and get them the hell out of Dodge. Zero tolerance: that's the policy we all have to enforce.

I know that in our family, Dave and I have always made it clear to our girls that they'd never see the light of day if they ever publicly threw a fit over something they wanted. (In fact, that was the exact language we used.) Once they were old enough to have legitimate conversations with us, we knew they were old enough to absorb what would happen if they ever acted that spoiled around other people. They'd be extracted from the situation before they had the chance to blink. Oh yeah, and we also used to remind them that if they acted badly around other people, we'd be embarrassing them the first chance we got. You know, mortification disguised as a "teachable moment."

Here's the thing: if someone else has something sparkly or blinky or pretty or cool looking, our kids want it. Since the beginning of time, people have coveted what other people have, especially kids. And in most cases, the average little kid will see absolutely no reason why they can't have the Tonka truck or the Presidential Barbie doll. So it takes a reeeeeeally long time and a lot of effort on our part to change that thinking. But it *is* possible. We just need to resign ourselves, upfront, to the fact that it's going to be an exhausting battle and that we're going to take a lot of direct hits to the metaphorical groin before it's over.

The other thing to keep in mind is that the earlier we teach our kids to be satisfied and content with what they have, the easier it is for us on the back end as they get older and want fancier and more expensive things.

Remember, the more they grow, the more in tune our kids become with what everyone around them has. They start paying very acute attention to what their friends are wearing and playing with and getting to do. And that's because they're moving further out in the world and they're getting exposed to more and more of what the world has to offer. Especially in the way of stuff.

When my girls were in the early elementary grades, they were no different than any of the other kids. They'd come home daily asking for things, in spite of our best efforts to teach them to be content. And even though they weren't asking for things like toys every day—maybe it was just ice cream or candy or to go to the movies—there'd always be some kind of *ask*. And the older they got, the bigger the ask became.

Trust me, we've cycled through all the fads of the month, like the black athletic tube socks that they both *just had to have*, the iPhones, the Ugg boots, the North Face fleeces, the Razor scooters, the Nintendo DS. Every generation has their own trends, and even though the stuff itself might be different, their desire for whatever the white-hot thing is at the moment is still insatiable.

And the wanting isn't just relegated to physical stuff. Our kids will also want the intangible things, like the same curfew their friends have or the same TV and gaming time their friends get or a bigger allowance. It never really stops. So it's up to us to teach them to be satisfied with what they have.

Everyone wants. It's just part of how we're all fundamentally wired. I mean, if that weren't the case, the word *covet* would never have been put in the Ten Commandments in the first place. But it's there. And it's there for a reason. Because, technically, according to The Big Guy, we're not supposed to want what other people have. Yeah, OK, right. In theory, maybe. But the reality is that we still do, whether we're supposed to or not.

And wanting things can be a pretty useful motivational tool

when used selectively with our kids. You know, as incentives. Like having a backyard campout when our kids keep their rooms clean all week. Or getting a little extra computer time when they finish all their homework. Or going bowling with friends if they do all their chores around the house. Because we all know those are things they want.

Who doesn't remember those feelings of desperately wanting something when we were kids? That need to have something sooooo badly that we could barely breathe or think about anything else? (*Obsession*, I believe it's called.) I can remember being so preoccupied when I got something stuck in my head that I became consumed by it, to the point of nauseating my parents. All kids do it. But that's normal.

Case in point: When I was around seven or eight, I vividly remember becoming hyperaware of the fact that most of my friends had dogs. They had snuggly, cuddly, deliciously sweet built-in playmates 24/7. And I wanted one too. It didn't take me very long to start campaigning to my parents to get one. And like most kids with an agenda, I campaigned hard.

In my young and naïve brain, I saw no good reason why we shouldn't have a family dog. And I was absolutely sure that I was doing my parents a huge favor by suggesting that we get one. Never mind the fact that my mom was *not* a dog person. Or that our house was empty during the day because both my parents worked. Or that our yard wasn't fenced in. I got dog in my head and couldn't get it out.

As a result, I wore my poor parents down to nubs, begging and pleading for a dog every time I opened my mouth. And while I don't remember exactly how long I hounded them, I know it went on for a while, because eventually, they gave in.

And that's what we do a lot of the time. We give in. Even when we're reluctant. Even when we have buckets full of reasons why we shouldn't. Sometimes we just do. Because as hard as it is for kids to learn how to accept *no* for an answer, it's just as hard for us to learn how to say it.

And that's because parenting isn't an exact science. No aspect of it. It's often really, really hard to know when to say yes or to say no or to intervene or to back away. Which is why we all screw up so much of the time with the decisions we make. And since most of the choices we make involving our kids are almost always motivated by their happiness and well-being, we sometimes cave and do stuff we know we shouldn't do just because we love them. Which is exactly why my parents let me have Murphy.

But don't assume that just because I ended up with a dog that I got everything I wanted growing up. Au contraire. And neither have my kids. My mom and dad said no when they had to, and so do we. We learned early the importance of teaching our kids that they can't have everything they want. And I'll tell you right now exactly how we learned it—we watched other young kids and their parents very carefully when our kids were growing up.

We paid close attention to the whiners and the pushover parents and made mental notes about the kinds of kids we did and *didn't* want to raise. Because, believe me, the spoiled brats of the world stood out like they were dressed in neon with Christmas lights all over them. And so did their parents. They served as good reminders of what *not* to do. Like how we can't give in to everything our kids ask for for the simple fact that people need limits. Especially little people.

I mean, none of us wants to see our kids sad—let alone to be the reason why they're sad. But the plain and simple fact of life is that we can't always give them what they want. Trust me; it's a terrible idea. Because to raise our kids to believe that they can or should get everything is just giving them unrealistic expectations. Once they're older, they'll realize pretty quickly that the rest of the world isn't going to accommodate them, even if mommy and daddy do.

Working around kids for so long, I constantly see kids who are rarely, if ever, denied anything by their parents. And believe me—it's nasty looking. You've seen them at the mall, or in the supermarket, or at the park; the kids who throw fits whenever they don't get what they want. Well, they're behaving that way because they're probably used to getting everything they ask for at home. So they just naturally assume that life functions that way outside the house too. OK, maybe not the little kids who are still learning to comprehend what *no* means, but when you see a grammar-school-age kid throwing a hissy in the candy store because he just won't leave without the baseball-size jawbreaker, that's a problem. A problem that's got to be nipped in the ol' bud before it gets out of control.

I mean, it's OK to want things. And with kids, it's expected. But there *has* to come a point when our kids accept the fact that (a) we're not a black hole filled with $50s and $100s, (b) it's unhealthy to get everything they ask for, and (c) they need to learn to get comfortable with disappointment because it's always going to be out there. But all these epiphanies take time for them to absorb. Which means that until they do, we have to be super diligent in reinforcing it every chance we get.

And we also *have* to have a strategy, like we do with every other stage with our kids. We have to get them accustomed to us asserting ourselves as their parents. Even though we're the ones they go to for love and support and reassurance, we have to remember that we're still the long arm of the law in our family. Because as much as they need us to be all of those things, they need us to set limits and enforce them. And we've got to be consistent. How they react to the limits we set is on them. When they start crying or throwing stuff or arguing with us, that's on them. When they try to manipulate us to get what they want, that's on them.

So the way we teach this concept is the exact same way we teach every concept to our kids. We hammer it over and over and over again. And then we hold the line tight with both hands and don't let go. (OK, maybe we loosen our grip once in a while, but not more than that.) Because even though we're the ones who really need to stick to the rules we make, we are allowed to bend them from time to time. It's called being flexible and making situational decisions. Like if our kids are bugging us to stay up an extra hour and we say no and then they bug us some more and we still say no, we reserve the right to make a compromise. We can say ten more minutes and they can either be OK with it or go to bed. Giving in to our kids and what they want really only does one thing . . . it reinforces that they're entitled to whatever they're trying to get. And that's the last thing we wanna do.

Also important here is the fact that our kids model how we act around them. If we have outbursts, it's likely that they'll do the same. If we're calm the majority of the time when we're dealing with them and their endless requests, then chances are good that they'll pick up on our vibe eventually.

And it's hard to stay that course when we've heard the same requests for stuff over and over. It wears us down. Yet when we lay it down with our kids and then just walk away, it's almost always a better outcome than getting into a debate with a raging six-year-old about why they can't have the Barbie camper that their best friend has. I've said "no" to my kids and then let myself go 'round and 'round with them when they pushed back, but the times that I laid it down and just left the room were the most successful.

The big mistake a lot of us make over and over is trying to calmly reason with a kid who's been alive for as many years as we have fingers on one hand. It. Doesn't. Work. Like when my girls were finally old enough to sit in the front seat of the car and they automatically assumed that they had control over the radio. They'd ask to listen to whatever the hot pop station was, and most of the time, I'd say yes. But not when anything from the '80s came on. Then I'd say no. And inevitably, I'd get some kind of attitude. To which I'd sometimes respond by snapping at them that I was just as entitled to choose what we listened to as they were. (Hell, I'm the one who owns the damn car.) But that was like lighting a stick of dynamite. Predictably, that would cause an exchange. And not the good kind. Blood would boil (usually mine), and someone's bottom lip would come out. Then verbal punches were thrown. Not effective.

But what almost always worked is when I gave the ultimatum that we either listen to *Come on Eileen* without anyone complaining or the radio goes off and we live in silence. And when I'd hear so much as an odd-sounding sniff from one of them, I'd smack that power button off and just smile. Worked like a charm.

The moral here is that we're the authoritarians. Period. And it's our kids' job to come to terms with that in their own way and at their own speed.

One other thing that really helps our kids absorb that no means no and that limits are actually a good thing is when we, ourselves, model that in our own lives. Especially when we do it around our kids.

Sure, we're the income-earning grown-ups who can, in theory, buy whatever stuff we want without needing to give anyone an explanation. But when our kids are young and we're teaching them that they can't have everything they want, we need to consciously rein ourselves in to prove the point. Because us buying whatever we want for ourselves sends a slightly hypocritical message to our kids. So if we practice what we preach, that modeling goes a long, long way toward proving that argument.

I know it's super tempting sometimes just to give in and give our kids what they want, but it's honestly one of the worst parenting mistakes we can ever make. Ever. Because once we bleed our hand and show them that they do actually have the power to manipulate us, they'll use that power to their advantage every chance they get. It's a classic good-versus-evil dilemma.

As the grown-ups, we all desperately want to keep the peace, and sometimes that urge makes us do crazy things, just like wanting the hottest new toy can make our kids go mental and behave like irrational lunatics. How many times have we put the Disney movie on one more time just to avoid the meltdown so we could make our three o'clock conference call without having a wild animal screaming at us in the background? Or shoved the extra handful of Halloween candy in our kid's face just to ensure that the last twenty miles of the five-hundred-mile road trip were in silence?

I've done it. You've done it. We've all had those frantic moments when we just needed to make them stop. So we can't beat ourselves up too badly when they happen. We just need to try to keep the win column fuller than the loss column. Our kids will thank us somewhere down the line, when they finally grow up and reflect back on the fact that they're not jerks, like a lot of other people out there. Guaranteed.

Myth #18

Myth: Our kids are born prewired with their temperament and attitude.

Reality: Our kids are a product of their environment.

If all of us had to pick one wish for our kids in their lifetime, I'll bet the majority of us would wish for them to be happy. I know I would. (In fact, it's the one thing I've always wished for my girls.) Because, at the end of the day, our ultimate goal in raising our kids is to raise healthy, *happy* little people who grow up to be content and positive grown-ups—grown-ups who can then take what they learned from us, put their own unique and beautiful spin on it, and pay it forward to their own families someday. And so on, and so on.

But that sense of happiness has to start somewhere. It has to be implanted, or rather imparted, by someone. We're not born with it. It's a state of being that we have to be exposed to, taught, and then given the opportunity to practice. Often. Most importantly, though, someone needs to explain to us that happiness is actually a choice—probably one of the most important choices any of us can make. And just like any other skill, like kindness or empathy or compassion, happiness is something that we need to learn. Because as far as I'm concerned, happiness is a life skill—a skill we learn first at home. And it starts with us. In fact, teaching it to our kids and then helping them hone it is one hundred percent our responsibility.

My kids have grown up hearing me say over and over how attitude is literally *everything*. That our attitude is one of the few things in life that we have complete control over. It's that one thing that isn't dependent on anyone else—the one thing we almost always have the ability to choose.

Like when we go to work every day, we can either choose to embrace the job we have to do and consciously give our best effort or choose to be negative and depressing and pessimistic. It's a pretty powerful concept once our kids are really old enough to embrace the idea.

When they're young, though, all we can do is keep reinforcing the simple idea that they can choose to make themselves miserable or allow themselves be happy in any given situation. (Not easy, even as simple as it sounds here in black and white.) And we need to emphasize it every chance we get. That's because it takes a long, long time before our kids develop a consistently positive outlook that enables them to squash their tendency to be negative and pouty.

Our kids can be upset that they're leaving the park or happy that they got to stay as long as they did. They can be mad that it's time to go to bed or happy that we're going to snuggle with them and read them a bedtime story. And it's our job to keep showing them the positive angle, because they're all just a little too young right now to see it for themselves. But they do get there. Ultimately, they do figure out that **positivity is like a superpower**—almost like having a shield that can repel just about anything negative. We just have to teach them how to use it.

I know with my own girls, I had to constantly remind them that having a positive attitude makes life easier all around. (Not an easy concept for young kids to grasp.) Like whenever one of my kids would come home in a bad mood from school or had a fight with a friend or tanked a test, and they'd let that bad mood fester and grow until it took over the entire mood in the house. Happened all the time. And I'd try to calm them down and make them see that being upset about something they couldn't change served no purpose. (Which worked about two percent of the time.)

I used to explain to my girls that they were always entitled to be sad or mad or frustrated about something as long as they worked through it and got to the other side. Because holding onto negativity does only one thing—it triggers more negativity. And I'd see it all the time in our house. When one of my kids was in a nasty mood, it always managed to permeate the rest of the house. One person would snap at someone, and then it became a domino effect. Everybody would start snapping, and before we knew it, there was a seismic mood shift in the house and everyone was nasty.

Fortunately, though, happiness works the exact same way for the simple reason that it's uplifting, positive, and feels good to be around.

I'm a big believer that happiness has a trickle-down effect, especially in families. It starts from the top—from us—and trickles its way through everyone else. Which is exactly why it's so critical that we model happiness early on with our kids. Kids tend to follow our lead with most things, after all.

So, there it is: **happy parents breed happy kids**. (In most cases.) And unhappy parents breed unhappy kids.

Now, sure, genetics represent an awful lot as far as prede-termining who we are physically and emotionally, but I also feel strongly that we're big products of where we come from. I mean, it's simple math that if a child comes from a troubled home, the likelihood of that same kid being troubled them-selves is high. And, on the flip side, it's just as logical to assume that a child who comes from a happy, loving, supportive home stands a better-than-average chance of becoming a well-adjust-ed, happy adult. And I believe it because I've seen the equation play out both ways firsthand.

I've lost count of the number of troubled kids who spent day after day in the principal's office with behavioral issues that stemmed from having no real parental involvement in their lives. They had no one holding them accountable for things like homework or behavior or attitude, and as a result, the kids roamed all over town, making bad choices, getting into trouble, and acting out. And it's sad. Because the parents, or at least the ones I'm thinking of in particular, couldn't be bothered to come to school to meet with our vice principal or their kid's teachers. They avoided getting involved with their kid's school. They avoided interacting with him at home. And their kid paid the price. He became an angry, unhappy person who had no idea that happiness was even an option.

See, without a parent or some kind of parental figure to guide or inspire or teach our kids that their attitude can be one of their most important assets, they just won't learn it. Because that's what it takes. It takes consistency and dedication. You know, because it's a labor of love. We need to constantly work at reinforcing those positive behaviors as much as we need to reinforce that they can't pee in their pants or pull someone's hair or sass-talk.

Sadly, though, I see examples of hands-off parenting every day. The kind of disconnected parenting that breeds unhappy, unloved, and unmotivated kids. I'm talking about moms and dads who staff out the responsibility of raising their kids even though they don't work and could be home caring for their own children. The ones who choose to be uninvolved, both emotionally or physically, in the day-to-day life of their kids. Parents who hire or enlist or line up someone else to do it for them. Parents who don't take the time to teach their kids how to think positively or build relationships or manage conflict or be gracious or kind or optimistic. Because this stuff can't be farmed out. Our kids have to learn all that knowledge from us. Not a nanny or a babysitter or an after-school program coach. Us. (NOTE: I'm *not* talking about the dual-income parents who have no choice but to secure childcare. They just have to be more creative in carving out the time to teach their kids.)

And, on the complete opposite hand, I've watched kids come into school every day who always projected happiness and contentment because they had parents who encouraged it. Every day. In school, on the playing field, at home. Everywhere. These were the kids whose attitude was so consistently positive and upbeat simply because they had someone guiding them at home, modeling the same kind of outlook. Practicing it with them day after day.

Now, I don't know about you, but I had kids because I wanted to raise them myself, to the best of my ability, so they could be the best people they had the capacity to be when they grew up. I didn't have kids so that someone else could take care of them. I didn't have kids so that someone else could discipline them. And I didn't have kids so that someone else could nurture and love them. Unfortunately, not everyone feels that way. There are too many parents out there who are way too quick to avoid putting in the real time and effort that it takes to bring up healthy, happy kids.

It's like I've said: happiness is a skill. It's something we all have to be taught. Like our numbers and letters and manners. And there's no denying that the process of building those skills into our hardwiring takes time and patience. Because it does. But in the same way that we have to hang onto the back of our kid's bike seat while they're learning to ride without training wheels, we have to nurture our kid's happiness too. Eventually, though, we get to let go.

Eventually, with time, our kids develop the bandwidth to understand that they can almost always choose happiness. In any situation. At school, with friends, on the soccer field. Everywhere. And when they make that conscious choice to stay focused on the positive side of a situation, they'll always be in control. It's almost like having a built-in personal floatation device (PFD) with them everywhere they go that ensures that they always stay buoyant, even when they're weighed down by negativity around them.

Remember . . .

Happy kids are motivated kids.

Happy kids are more productive kids.

Happy kids are more expressive kids.

Happy kids are more communicative kids.

Happy kids are more fulfilled kids.

Happy kids are more empowered kids.

You know as well as I do how much negativity there is out there. And no one's immune to it. We've all had to work with the woman who was constantly complaining about her dead-end job or her unhappy marriage or her pain-in-the-butt kids or her deadbeat husband. There's definitely a population of people out there who somehow seem happier when they have something to complain about. Which has to be exhausting. They're the people you try to hide from when you see them coming down the hall. The ones who focus almost exclusively on the dark, negative side of everything.

Personally, I find negativity toxic and a complete turnoff, as far as qualities go. Now, sure, we're all entitled to have episodes or periods of sadness or unhappiness or discontent—because that's just life—but when those moments develop into a regular pattern of behavior, then we've got a problem. And our kids pick up on it. Like the mom of one of my daughter Riley's friends who used to trash-talk her kid to me every chance she got. Privately, to me, and in front of her daughter. And it was gross. Because her daughter felt the punch of negativity every time a hurtful word came out of her mom's mouth. And her mom just could never manage to find something positive to say to her daughter, which was agonizing to watch up close. The daughter was a hard worker with a good work ethic and good people skills, but you could see her totally deflate every time her mom hurled negativity at her. And as a result, the older the girl got, the more prone she became to hurling the same negativity at her own friends. She became a product of her environment.

My point is, we're all a product of where we come from—especially our kids. And if we aspire to raise well-adjusted and happy kids, then we have to create that kind of environment for them at home. And we have to support it by being positive ourselves. We can't just walk around saying one thing and doing another. We can't drone on about doing the food shopping or the ironing or the lawn every week and then expect our kids to willingly and happily sit down and do their math homework. We need to walk the walk and talk the talk ourselves. Otherwise everything we're doing is a sham.

It's just not possible to teach our kids how to be joyful unless we're happy ourselves. We're the single most powerful role models for happiness that our kids will ever have. So if we don't project authentic happiness and contentment, then our kids will never learn to do it themselves. If we're constantly whiny and intolerant and judgmental, then we should naturally assume that that behavior will rub off on our kids. So we need to watch ourselves and how we behave around them. We need to keep our moods in check and stay conscious of the attitude that we project. Because our kids are watching and absorbing and copying and regurgitating.

I know that in the case of my own childhood, my mother had an awful lot she could've been down about, considering she was suddenly widowed at forty with a ten-year-old daughter at home. She could've been mad at her situation, depressed, foul, even, and no one would've blamed her under the circumstances. And that anger or disappointment or feeling of being overwhelmed could have easily filtered down to me. But it didn't. She didn't allow it. She stayed positive in the face of extreme loss and pushed on. And while she never hid her sadness, she made sure it was heavily tempered by her ability to still focus on all the positive pieces of her life. Of our life. She did little things like sing or hum all the time. Still does. I was constantly being hugged and kissed and cuddled and smiled at. She made an effort to see the positive side in everything. And she made sure that I knew that even though there is extreme sadness and disappointment in life, it's balanced by immense joy and beauty and happiness.

And that's what I'm talking about. I'm talking about the fact that molding who our children are and how they perceive and interact with the world is our job and happens under our roof. Who our kids become is a direct result of our effort and commitment. So we need to make sure that they understand, from as early on as possible, that everything we say or do in our lives can almost always go one of two ways: positive or negative. We can see the cup as half full or half empty. The perspective we choose to take is up to us.

The irony is that as desperately as we all want to raise our kids to be happy and joyful, we have to also raise them to accept the reality that life isn't always that big, overflowing bowl of cherries. That there's disappointment woven into every phase of life.

We have to remember that life is mixed with a wide range of emotions and the only way to ensure that our kids are prepared for what's out there is to let them experience as many of them as possible. That means they have to experience the highs as well as the lows. Because the only way to really ensure that our kids know how to handle certain things is to actually let them experience the widest range of emotions we can. We can't insulate them from the life around them. Our kids need to feel the pain and the bliss and the success and the disappointment that's out there in life in order to learn how to navigate through it when the time comes.

The simple, unfiltered truth is that life and parenthood are not straight lines. But armed with a positive attitude and a foundation of happiness, love, and support, our kids will have the tools they need to grow into healthy, happy, well-adjusted teens and young adults—and eventually grown-ups and parents themselves. And we can sleep well at night knowing that we gave them the most important tools parents can give their kids to ensure they can build themselves a successful, happy life.

Because we're only as happy as our least happy kid.

Just a Sec . . . We're Not Quite Done Yet

This first book in the *Untying Parent Anxiety* series may be over, but we both know that there's an awful lot more still to come. These initial few years in school are followed, of course, by many, many more. And with each age and grade comes new and different challenges. Unfortunately, though, there's no one proven way to handle them all.

Because bringing up kids is more or less baptism by fire. So all we can do as moms and dads is remember that parenthood is a work in progress and not be afraid to try and fail and try again. Because to fixate on raising the perfect kid is a waste of time. It's not going to happen. Instead, we need to embrace our imperfections—and theirs—and keep in mind that life is not a straight line.

That's why I'm writing three more books to talk, in depth, about each stage—a book a year for the next three years—designed to pacify the anxious parent.

- *Untying Parent Anxiety (Ages 9–12)*
- *Untying Parent Anxiety (Ages 13–16)*
- *Untying Parent Anxiety (Ages 17–20)*

Want to ensure that you don't miss the next one? Visit my website at **www.lisasugarman.com** and sign up for my mailing list. It's that easy. And while you're waiting for the launch of my next book, you'll get my nationally syndicated humor column *It Is What It Is* in your inbox every week. You know, just to keep you entertained.

Afterword

When Dave and I started our family almost twenty years ago, we were more or less clueless about how to be parents. We had only been married for four years, so we were basically kids ourselves, and even though we had our own parents and family nearby to help guide us, the ultimate responsibility of figuring it out was on us.

Sure, we read plenty of parenting books, and all of them helped to give us at least a vague sense of what to expect in terms of the major growth and development stages. But there was nothing out there that talked honestly, in an unfiltered way, about all the *other* stuff that goes along with being a parent. You know, the stuff like kid drama and participation trophies and how it feels when our kids start giving us attitude for the first time or what it's like the first time we get a door slammed in our face.

I'd like to say that after a lot of failed attempts, we found a rhythm. And in a lot of ways, we did. We got used to having a little person in tow all the time and always sleeping with one ear open. We got comfortable putting our daughters' best interests ahead of our own. We learned that it's way easier to make five salami sandwiches on Sunday afternoon and freeze them for the week than it is to get up early to make a sandwich every morning before school. We learned that when you say your piece to your kid during a conflict and then walk away, it usually causes them to come to you first to apologize.

But we also learned that so much of parenting is subjective and freeform and unpredictable. That no matter how badly we wanted our kids to be happy all the time, life just didn't work that way. We learned that just because a discipline strategy worked for one family didn't mean it would work across the board. We figured out that we have to let our kids fail and fall and be sad because those are some of life's greatest lessons. Because when we fall and get up again or when we're sad and find happiness again, we appreciate it all the more.

We came to realize that our kids were going to find their niche and their "crowd" and their way by tons of trial and error. But they found it. We learned that all the best-laid plans and hopes and dreams we had for our kids were usually very different from how things actually turned out, so we had to be nimble and adaptable and open minded.

The most important thing we learned, though, was that no family is perfect, no matter how hard we all try. We're not always going to get it right, and our kids aren't always going to be the model little citizens we want them to be—because we're all a work in progress.

And that was a super powerful nugget of parenting truth—so powerful that I started writing about it in my nationally syndicated opinion/humor column *It Is What It Is*. And people everywhere started responding to the idea, saying it gave them the reality check they needed to loosen up and dial down their expectations for perfection. Readers told me that once they stopped expecting their kids to be perfect and just let them be kids, there was a noticeable shift in the family dynamic for the better. So I kept writing, and people kept responding.

Then **Familius** and I found each other and realized that we had the same mission of making families happy. So I pitched them an idea for a book about how to raise perfectly imperfect kids and be okay with it (ironically, at the exact time that we sent our first daughter off to college). And instead of giving the thumbs up to that one book, they decided it made more sense as a four-book series that followed our kids from kindergarten through college. And *bam*—here we are.

That's how *Untying Parent Anxiety* came to be.

So hang tight, because there's a lot more still to come. Books Two, Three, and Four are already in the works. And I'm writing as fast as I can.

Sources

1. Child Mind Institute. *2016 Children's Mental Health Report.* http://childmind.org/report/2016-childrens-mental-health-report/.

2. YoungMinds.org. "Mental Health Statistics." Accessed September 26, 2016. http://www.youngminds.org.uk/training_services/policy/mental_health_statistics.

3. Fulghum, Robert. *All I Really Need to Know I Learned in Kindergarten.* New York: Ballantine Books, 2004.

4. Resnick, Mitchel. "Kindergarten is the Model for Lifelong Learning." Edutopia.org. May 27, 2009. http://www.edutopia.org/kindergarten-creativity-collaboration-lifelong-learning.

5. "The Synapse." Neuroscience for Kids. Accessed September 26, 2016. https://faculty.washington.edu/chudler/synapse.html.

6. Hirsh-Pasek, Kathy, and Roberta Michnick Golinkoff. *Einstein Never Used Flashcards: How Our Children Really Learn—and Why They Need to Play More and Memorize Less.* Emmaus, PA: Rodale, 2003.

7. Scholastic.com. "The Joys of Doing Nothing." Accessed September 26th, 2016. http://www.scholastic.com/parents/resources/article/creativity-play/joys-doing-nothing.

8. Brenner, Joel. "Sports Specialization and Intensive Training in Young Athletes." American Academy of Pediatrics. August 2016. http://pediatrics.aappublications.org/content/early/2016/08/25/peds.2016-2148.

9. Chin, Richard. "The Science of Sarcasm? Yeah, Right." Smithosonian.com. November 14, 2011. http://www.smithsonianmag.com/science-nature/the-science-of-sarcasm-yeah-right-25038/?no-ist.

10. Ibid.

11. KidsHealth.org. "Encouraging Your Child's Sense of Humor." Accessed September 26, 2016. http://kidshealth.org/en/parents/child-humor.html.

12. Fluckey, Eric. "Why Sarcasm Is So Great." *Huffington Post*. Last updated August 4, 2016. http://www.huffingtonpost.com/eric-fluckey/why-sarcasm-is-so-great_b_7887342.html.

13. Scribner, Herb. "Most American Children Have a Cell Phone Before They Turn 7 Years Old." *Deseret News National*. April 7, 2015. http://national.deseretnews.com/article/4005/most-american-children-have-a-cell-phone-before-they-turn-7-years-old.html.

14. DiProperzio, Linda. "Creative Ways to Teach Sharing." Parents.com. Accessed September 26, 2016. http://www.parents.com/toddlers-preschoolers/development/social/ways-to-teach-sharing/.

15. Durlofsky, Paula. "The Benefits of Emotional Intelligence." PsychCentral.com. Accessed September 26, 2016. http://psychcentral.com/blog/archives/2015/10/29/the-benefits-of-emotional-intelligence/.

16. Bradberry, Travis. "Emotional Intelligence—EQ." Forbes.com. January 9, 2014. http://www.forbes.com/sites/travisbradberry/2014/01/09/emotional-intelligence/#1ed6d0f93ecb.

17. Jensen, Keld. "Intelligence Is Overrated: What You Really Need to Succeed." Forbes.com. April 12, 2012. http://www.forbes.com/sites/keldjensen/2012/04/12/intelligence-is-overrated-what-you-really-need-to-succeed/#7e2433cd6375.

18. Ibid.

About the Author

LISA SUGARMAN is the author of the nationally syndicated opinion column *It Is What It Is*, featured in over five hundred GateHouse Media, Inc. newspapers and websites around the country.

She is also a long-time columnist and humorist for GateHouse as well as a regular contributor to LittleThings.com, BeingaMom.life, and *Active Family Magazine*. The mother of two, running coach, wife, and author understands firsthand that we can't control everything that life throws at us—but we *can* control how we react to it.

She reminds us that it's only when we realize that life isn't a straight line that we can truly find happiness.

"Life is messy and unpredictable. The bottom line," she says, "is that we're designed to screw up, make bad decisions, and lose our way. Because the reality is that life isn't perfect; it's often messy, chaotic, and sometimes downright mean. But it's also joyous, fulfilling, and endlessly surprising. We just have to remember that it's a work in progress."

Lisa is also the author of the *Boston Globe* local best-seller *LIFE: It Is What It Is*, a collection of her fifty favorite *It Is What It Is* opinion columns, available on Amazon, on Barnes&Noble.com, at all Hugo Bookstores, and at select Whole Foods Market stores. She has also made frequent radio appearances from coast to coast. Some of her radio appearances include *Thank God for Mondays, The Warren Lawrence Show, Talk of the Town, The Brynn Project, The Experience Pros, Morning Magazine, KPQ News Reports,* and *Midday Café with Jack Baldwin.*

About Familius

VISIT OUR WEBSITE: www.familius.com

JOIN OUR FAMILY: There are lots of ways to connect with us! Subscribe to our newsletters at www.familius.com to receive uplifting daily inspiration, essays from our Pater Familius, a free ebook every month, and the first word on special discounts and Familius news.

GET BULK DISCOUNTS: If you feel a few friends and family might benefit from what you've read, let us know and we'll be happy to provide you with quantity discounts. Simply email us at orders@familius.com.

CONNECT:
www.facebook.com/paterfamilius
@familiustalk, @paterfamilius1
www.pinterest.com/familius

FAMILIUS

The most important work
you ever do will be within
the walls of your own home.

CPSIA information can be obtained
at www.ICGtesting.com
Printed in the USA
FSOW01n1834250117
30000FS